DETOUR
THROUGH
HELL

DANNY VELASCO

Published by Salon Success Systems 2014

Book cover design and formatting services by www.BookCoverCafe.com

First Edition 2014

978-0-578-03025-8 (pbk)
978-0-615-96910-7 (ebk)

ABOUT THE AUTHOR

 **Danny Velasco**: For nearly 40 years, Danny's career took him around the world as a freelance Hairdresser and Makeup Artist to Fashion Models, Celebrities, and Rock Stars. His work has appeared the covers of Vogue, Bazaar, Cosmopolitan, Marie Claire, Elle, and many other fashion magazines throughout the US and Europe. The story of Danny's amazing transformation has been featured on:

The 700 Club

Billy Graham Association "Decision Today"

Campus Crusade for Christ

"Breakthrough Prayer" by Pastor Jim Cymbala

"When God's People Pray" by Pastor Jim Cymbala

"I'm Amazed" DVD

"This Is Your House" CD

Christian Women Today

Men Today Online

"Transformation" (WMCA, 570AM, New York's Christian Radio)

CBN Website

Revive Magazine

Global Christian Network (Korea and World Wide)

Danny was the Director of Celebrate Recovery Ministry for the Brooklyn Tabernacle Church, an outreach that helps people with habits, hurts, and hang-ups.

Please visit **www.DetourThroughHell.org** to watch Danny's online videos, read articles, listen and download his audio testimony so you can share his story with those in need.

Praise for DETOUR THROUGH HELL

"I have heard hundreds of stories of God's transformation power at work in people's lives but Danny's story is the most amazing and encouraging one of them all. From the height of success in our business to living on the streets of New York without a home, we watched this story unfold. The faithful prayers and witness of one of our models, Wanda, is also an awesome example of how God can use each of us right where we are.

I was blessed to know Danny, now transformed by God's grace and power. His story is one you will never forget."

— *JEFF CALENBERG*, *Model/Photographer/Founder of Models for Christ*

"It was my privilege to translate for Danny Velasco as he shared his amazing story with thousands of Japanese in various cities of Japan. Danny's modern day, life-changing miracle is another universal tribute to the unchanging power of Jesus Christ. The reality of his experience crosses all cultural and language barriers and will inspire anyone, in any sphere of life."

— *STEVEN KAYLOR*, *Pastor of Hope Church, Tokyo, Japan*

"Reads like a novel, but resonates God's truth, love, and grace."

— *MARGARET SCOTT/TISH CRAIG*, *Transformation Ministries, WMCA RADIO/570AM*

"Danny's story is one of the many amazing testimonies to come from The Brooklyn Tabernacle in New York City. He was a living example of a total transformation when one decides to change their lifestyle and refuses to compromise. God's "Amazing Grace" is real and more than mere lyrics to a famous song. His story is true and I pray it will bring Hope and Redemption to many. "Let the redeemed of the Lord say so.""

— *MORRIS CHAPMAN*, *Singer, Songwriter, and Worship Leader*

Mercy is God not giving us what we deserve.
Grace is God giving us what we don't deserve.

—AUTHOR UNKNOWN

CONTENTS

FOREWORD

The conversion of Danny Velasco is a stirring story that reminds me of both Saul of Tarsus and Lazarus from the Bible.

From a sarcastic mocker of Christianity, Danny was transformed by the grace of God into an eloquent spokesman for the faith he once ridiculed.

After years of living homeless on the cruel streets of New York City, his emaciated, desperately ill body was raised up by Christ into a life of spiritual freedom.

Danny Velasco was a walking and talking miracle of God!

As his pastor, I watched Danny inspire audiences around the world with his sincere testimony of God's grace. What a wonderful reminder he was that God's power has never changed across all the centuries of history. The Gospel of Christ is still "the power of God for the salvation of everyone who believes" (Romans 1:16.) How else can one explain the transformation of this man?

Danny's life also reminds us that God's heart is full of mercy. In a day when many give up praying because the situation seems hopeless, Danny Velasco stands as a trophy of the longsuffering and kindness of our heavenly Father.

You will be deeply moved and never forget the story you are about to read.

JIM CYMBALA
Senior Pastor
The Brooklyn Tabernacle, Brooklyn, N.Y.

ACKNOWLEDGEMENTS

I would like to take this opportunity to thank so many people who have been so kind to me over the years as I walk this path. There are so many that I could never really thank everyone so if your name is not here, please know that I love you with all my heart and cherish your friendship.

I would like to start with thanking Wanda Geddie Brickner for first telling me about the Good News, the Gospel of Jesus Christ. Your bold witness has changed my life forever. I am eternally grateful ... Ward, you have been a good friend. Thank you.

Liz Silvestri, you were there from the beginning. Thanks for all the talks and late night bible discussions. I grew and grew because of the wisdom that you so readily gave.

Pam Sanders, thanks for being a great friend.

Pastor Jim Cymbala. Who could ask for a better Pastor than you? You have helped raise me up and believed God for me when I couldn't see my way through. You believed in me, encouraged me, and taught me. I always want to make you proud of me and because of you I strived to be better than I thought I could be.

Carol Cymbala, thank you for the privilege of allowing me to sing in your wonderful choir. I love worshipping the Lord and you have given me the chance to do it in song. (Even though I'm not the best singer around!) I'm always amazed.

My brother and sister-in-law, David and Cynthia Velasco, I love you so much. I am so thankful to God for you. And my two beautiful nieces, Bianca and Sienna, you are both a gift from heaven.

My agent and dear friend, Rosemary Bennett, I would like to thank you for all that you have done for me over the years and for always being there with me through the good times and bad.

Pastor Rick Johnson, thank you for your commitment and dedication to teaching and reaching out to the lost and broken. I cherish your friendship.

Reverend Dave and Jennett Sanders, when I had nowhere to go, you took me in. When I was hungry, you fed me and when I was thirsty, you gave me drink. What you have done for the least of us, you have done unto the Lord. Thank you.

Roger and Mary Skinner, you are like a brother and sister to me. You are good friends. You took me into your family and treated me like family. I love you both.

To my Brooklyn Tabernacle family, you all mean so much to me. Over the years, I have watched you. Watching you has taught me how to walk, how to talk, how to love, how to accept, how to worship, how to pray. How could I ever thank you?

My life has been enriched by countless people. Today, as we all are, I am the total sum of all the experiences that I have had in life. Looking back, I happily accept every experience, both good and bad. They have made me who I am today.

I thank the Lord Jesus for all of them. He allowed me to have them, kept His hand of protection on me and now He shows me that all were necessary somehow in His plan and purpose for my life.

I pray that He will continue to give me the awesome opportunity to use them all for His Glory.

This book is dedicated to Elba and John Velasco, my mom and dad.

I would also like to dedicate it to Ethel (sister) Velasco and Bessie Gonzalez, my grandmother and great aunt, who were also like my mom and dad.

INTRODUCTION

It is a cold night in April, 1994. The cool air feels good on my face. I am 44 years old, homeless, and I weigh 108 pounds. My skeletal arms are covered with sores and abscesses. My shirtsleeves are stuck to my arms.

I have Hepatitis A, B, and C; my skin and eyes are yellow with jaundice.

Voices are screaming simultaneously in my head. One constantly accuses me and reminds me what a failure I am. A second voice yells a steady stream of filthy words. A third one just laughs mockingly.

I have numerous phobias that drive me and dictate where I can go and what I can do.

On this cold April night, I am sitting on a sidewalk in the Bronx, NY, leaning back against a building next to a garbage bin. Rats scurry by, but because my mind plays tricks on me, I don't know which ones are real and which ones aren't.

The building I am leaning against is a hospital. I am waiting to go inside to die. I don't want to die on the street, hunched against a trashcan with real and imaginary rats running around. I want to die in a clean, quiet hospital.

I have no ID on me. Nothing will reveal my identity. My family will never be called to identify my body.

I will be buried in a pauper's grave, and that will be the end of me.

My family will always wonder what happened to me, but at least they won't be left with their final memories of me like this.

Maybe they will remember me as I once was.

PART ONE
The Early Years

CHAPTER I

The Hurt Child

"When I was a child, I talked like a child, I thought like a child, I reasoned like a child."
1 CORINTHIANS 13:11

I looked around at all the clowns. Some were juggling, some riding on small bicycles, and others just clowning around. The lion tamer had a whip in one hand and a chair in the other. The lions were standing up on their hind legs, growling ferociously, their teeth showing.

Trapeze artists swung high against the backdrop of blue sky and white puffy clouds, their arms outstretched, ready to catch each other.

The year was 1955. I was five years old at the time. I snuggled deeper in my bed and pulled the covers up to my neck, feeling very secure. My mother had lovingly and painstakingly hand painted a circus scene on every wall of my room. Even the sky on the ceiling was painted with a lot of detail.

But something was wrong in our home. Something was going on that, given my young age, I didn't quite understand.

My mother had woken up one day with a butterfly rash on her face. We went to the hospital to have it checked. The doctor at the Gonzalez Clinic in Tampa, Florida, where we lived, took one look at her and his eyes widened.

"La Mariposa," he whispered, as if he had never expected to see this in person. The butterfly-shaped rash was the first sign of Systemic Lupus Erythematosus, better known simply as Lupus, an autoimmune disease characterized by inflammation in various parts of the body.

Later, other doctors not only confirmed the diagnosis but also discovered that mother was pregnant. Her doctors advised her to abort and immediately begin taking cortisone to counter the inflammation.

As if the mere discovery of this invasive illness were not bad enough, the doctors also told my mother that if the child was a girl, she too would have the disease or be stillborn.

My mother was a devout Catholic and refused to abort. She also refused the medication until the child was born. She was confined to her bed for the entire pregnancy.

All of my family chipped in to hire a full time nanny/housekeeper. An elderly black woman by the name of Thelma came to live with us. Thelma became my surrogate mother for the next couple of years.

After my healthy little brother, David, was born, mother began her cortisone treatments. The medication caused her face to swell into a large, round, moon-face that didn't look like my mother's. I watched as she grew weaker and weaker. When I came home from school, the door to her room would be closed. Our housekeeper, Thelma, was the one who helped with my homework and fed us.

After dinner, I was allowed to see my mother for a little while. I would climb up into her big bed and snuggle up to her. I remember that her perfume smelled like gardenias. She still looked beautiful to me.

My father had built a sliding, angled table for her to be able to read without holding the book up with her arms. Her Bible was always open and she would read a passage or two to me every night, usually something from the Book of Daniel or by King David. Those were the names of my baby brother and me. Mother knew I liked to hear our names in the Bible.

After a while, Thelma would shoo me out of the room, saying that my mother needed to rest. Each night after David and I were bathed, Thelma would put us to bed.

My father then helped my mother walk into our room and she would lay in bed with me and sing: "*Our Father, who art in heaven, hallowed be thy name…*" Sometimes I would drift off to sleep as her soft voice soothed away all my fears. I felt secure and loved as I dozed to my mother's voice, singing and humming. For the next few years, she mostly lay in bed and that was our routine. I was six, maybe seven, years old by then, and my baby brother was two. Priests from our local parish came to the house on Sunday afternoons after church services, along with three or four nuns, and they would hold a service in my mother's bedroom.

The priest would then hear my mother and father's confessions and serve communion. Afterwards, he would come into my bedroom and sit on one of the two twin beds. I would sit on the other one, holding a little piece of paper where my list of sins were carefully written, and read them off to him one by one. Then I would receive forgiveness and communion.

Much of what I remember about my childhood touches on these two facts—my mother was very sick and very religious. One of mother's last wishes was to visit as many world famous shrines as she could with whatever time she had left. She was like my "old" mother again, as I remember her walking on her knees to the Basilica of Nuestra Senora de Guadalupe in Mexico. Her knees were bloody when she reached the shrine, but she did it and she was happy.

My father had a second job with Eastern Airlines, which allowed our family to fly very inexpensively. When I was about eight years old, we flew to Lourdes, France. Many people over the years had been cured of every disease under the sun and my mother was sure that she, too, would be healed if she bathed in the shrine's waters.

I remember the day we arrived in Paris and took a train south to Lourdes. The following morning, we walked from our hotel to the shrine several blocks away. My mother was covered up as much as possible because her disease had caused a powerful allergy to the sun. It would burn her skin on contact, and she would get bad sores. Even though she was snugly covered, the lower parts of her legs were bleeding by the time we arrived at the shrine. I was young, but I stayed outside all by myself while my parents went inside and got in line with other believers hoping for a miracle of their own.

When my mother's turn came, she took a cup, dipped it in the water, and drank. This was the same water that hundreds maybe even thousands of people suffering from every imaginable disease bathed with and drank that very day. This must have boosted my mother's faith enormously.

Her belief was so strong that she bathed in the waters and afterwards emptied the medicine bottles that had been keeping her alive into the river that ran alongside the shrine.

Back home from France, my mother took to her bed again. She had no trace of lupus left in her body, but the disease had left her very weak. Our family announced the miracle to anyone who would listen.

One year later, to the day, on February 14, 1960, mother contracted a particularly dangerous strain of Hong Kong Flu and was hospitalized in Tampa General Hospital.

She was isolated because this particular strain was very contagious. I wasn't allowed to see her. My father used to take me to the front of the hospital, and I would stand outside with some relative or another while my father went up to the floor where Mother was. I looked up until I would see my father in a window. A few seconds later, my mother appeared, smiled, and waved at me. Then she would blow me a kiss.

I was very happy to see her because I missed her so much. Then she would disappear from the window. A while later, my father came out of the building, and we went home.

One night my father announced that my mother wasn't contagious anymore and that this night he was going to sneak me up a back staircase to see her. I walked in the room and saw her lying in bed, very weak and pale. She was also extremely thin. Father helped her sit up, held me up to her level, and I hugged and kissed her. Tears filled her eyes and I said, "Don't cry, Mommy. You're not sick anymore." She smiled and said, "I heard you learned a song at school. Let me hear it."

I went into my rendition of "I'm a Little Teacup," complete with hand and body moves. She smiled and clapped her hands. I climbed into the bed with her and cuddled.

Then she spoke to me: "Now, Danny, you and your baby brother have to always love each other. And when he gets older, I want you to take care of him. Teach him to tie his shoes and to dress himself. And when he goes to school, you walk with him on his first day, be there waiting for him when school lets out, and walk him home. Okay?"

"Okay," I said. I didn't really see how this was important, but it seemed to mean a lot to her.

Father said it was time to go, so we left the room. I couldn't have known it at the time, but that was the last time I saw my mother. She passed away a few hours later.

I remember my father, who was only in his twenties at that time, coming home from the hospital the next day. I was at my grandmother's house. My great-aunt had answered a phone call earlier in the day. When she hung up, all she could do was walk around the house and wring her hands. She looked very shaken.

My father came in at about 6 PM and took me into a back room. He sat down and hoisted me up on his lap.

"Do you know how much your mama loves Jesus?" he asked. "Well, she's gone to live with him in heaven."

I tried to process this information. My little mind (I was only nine at the time) was on overload. I remember not feeling sad. I was confused and I was angry at mother for wanting to live with Jesus rather than with us. I was also angry at my father for not being able to stop her. And I was angry with Jesus for taking her away.

"What are we going to do?" I finally asked.

"You and your little brother are going to live here with Granny and Aunt Bessie," he said. "I will still live at our house, until I decide what to do next. I will come by and see you every day, I promise."

My mind reeled. Life had changed. Nothing would ever be the same again. I wondered why dad allowed this to happen. And why did Jesus take mother away? Of course, I had no answers, but I felt confused and betrayed.

Nuns from St. Joseph's, our local parish, went to my father's house and cleared away all traces of my mother. My father kept his promise, and every day after work he would stop by and have dinner with us.

Not long after Mother died, Father Smith from St. Joseph's said to me, "You have to be strong now that your mother is gone, Danny."

"Will I see her in heaven?" I asked.

"Yes," he answered. "But your mother is not in heaven yet. She's in purgatory. She has to pay for her sins. Now, it's up to you to pray so that she has less time in purgatory. Each time you pray the 'Our Father Who Art in Heaven' and the 'Hail Mary Full of Grace,' you will take one day off her time in purgatory. So, you must pray all the time for her."

I started to pray fervently. I kept a record of how many times I said these prayers. I stopped walking to school with my friends, so that I could use this time to pray. I would pray on my way to and from school, and I would "speed pray" to get in as many prayers as I could manage to whisper.

After several weeks of this "prayer marathon," I decided to stop by the rectory and speak to Father Smith. I had questions that I needed answered.

The receptionist asked me to take a seat and wait. Sitting still was not easy for a nine-year-old boy, but I had very important matters to discuss with Father Smith.

Finally, he appeared and smiled. "Daniel, how can I help you?"

"How do you know when you have prayed enough?" I blurted out. "How will I know that they let mother out of purgatory and into heaven?"

Suddenly, his look became very serious. He sensed that these were very important questions and concerns for me. He looked down, thought for a moment, and finally turned to me and said, "You will never know, son. That is why you have to pray for her for the rest of your life. And that is why, when you get married and have kids, you have to bring them up in the Catholic Church so that they can pray for you when you die."

I left the rectory in a daze. Many thoughts rushed through my little brain. I decided that I would never pray again. I resented Jesus for taking my mother to live with him. I resented my mother for wanting to be with Jesus more than she wanted to be with me. And I also resented my father. Maybe he wasn't a good enough husband, I thought? The burden of such a great responsibility as making sure that my mother went to heaven weighed heavily on me. My eyes burned with tears. Anger made my heart beat faster and I began to run. I wanted to run until I dropped dead. Then I could be with my mother in that limbo-land called the purgatory. It might not be heaven, but at least we would be together.

After my mother's passing, my father was overwhelmed with medical bills that he could not pay. Our home at the time was a large Florida rancher with an efficiency apartment attached in the back. Eventually, my father moved into the efficiency apartment and rented out the main part of the house to help with the medical bills. All this time, my brother and I lived with our grandmother and Aunt Bessie. My father continued to visit us every day.

CHAPTER 2

The Cocky Teenager

"Vanity of vanities, all is vanity."
ECCLESIASTES 1:2

Fast-forward to the mid-1960s. I was a teenager. My father worked as a photographer for a large corporation and eventually met a beautiful red-haired divorcée named Doris.

Doris was a fun-loving, out-going Georgia girl who loved my father dearly and brought laughter back into our house. She also had two daughters from a previous marriage who were very close in age to my brother and me. We were like the Brady Bunch and got along great.

As it turned out, Doris and her daughters needed a place to live and my father needed a tenant. So, over the next few years during their long courtship, Doris and her daughters lived in the main part of the house while my father lived in the attached apartment. David and I continued to live with our grandmother.

Doris's daughters were enrolled in the same school as we were, and right away began to call my father "dad." I found it very strange because I would never be able to call their mother "mother." Don't get me wrong, I really liked her and she was very sweet to David and me (and devoted to my father, as well), but she was not my mother. I considered her my father's wife.

My father and Doris eventually did marry and David went to live with them, while I stayed with my grandmother and her sister, my great-aunt Bessie. They were like parents to me. My grandmother worked six days a week at my uncle's Venetian blind and drapery company. Bessie stayed at home and kept house.

Bessie was a sweet, gentle, and loving woman. My grandmother, on the other hand, was hardworking, but cold. I saw my father often, but he now had a new ready-made family to take care of. I always knew that he loved me, but he wanted to be more of a friend than a father to me. I called him Johnny.

I lived with my grandmother, but I was pretty much on my own at 14. In many ways, I was getting away with murder.

I earned money with a daily after-school paper route. On Saturdays, I would clean my uncle's Venetian blind shop and then go to the local barbershop to clean up there. I earned enough money to buy my own clothes and go out whenever and wherever I wanted. I was very popular at school and had a close-knit group of friends who were like a family to me. Staying out all weekend was no problem. I was told to just call and let grandmother and Bessie know I wasn't coming home.

I was a very cocky and arrogant teenager. If my grandmother or great-aunt ever questioned me about my whereabouts, I would tell them that it was none of their business. After a while, they just stopped asking.

My father never disciplined me either. He preferred being my friend and pretty much approved of anything I did. On one hand, it was great. I could talk to him about anything and everything. On the other hand, I lacked the parental guidance and supervision all teenagers need to stay out of trouble.

My friends loved my father and looked to him as an older brother. They could talk freely in front of him about things they wouldn't dare tell their own parents. They all thought I had the coolest father ever. It all seemed great to me at the time.

But, because he was my friend and let me live my life any way I chose, I grew up with no boundaries and no direction. Kids don't need their parents to be friends. They will have enough friends of their own. Kids need parents to be just that—parents.

Not having any parental influence in my life, I used to stay out all night, drink, smoke pot, and party. I was always pushing the boundaries a little further and never really found those invisible lines. They were never defined for me.

Tampa was a great place for a kid to grow up, but the times were different then. Segregation was still alive and in full swing in the

South. Martin Luther King had not yet started his peaceful protest for equal rights for Black Americans. Bathrooms and water fountains in my hometown (and across America) were still labeled C-Men and W-Men. Certain restaurants still wouldn't allow black customers.

My family was Cuban, and somehow we were stuck in the middle. We looked white, but too often we would hear comments about "spics" and "niggers." That was, of course, long before the notion of political correctness permeated the collective consciousness.

I went to elementary and middle school with all the other Hispanic kids in town. We were in a limbo—hanging between black and white and not accepted by either.

Racism was ugly and set people against each other. My father hated racism and segregation. Any sign of either was prohibited around him.

While I was in 10th grade, laws were passed, and we were forced to integrate. Black kids were sent to our high school according to the "zones" in which they lived. And my friends were scattered around as well.

Our first black student was a girl named Willie Ruth Calhoun. Her father was the Rev. Leroy Calhoun and we took her in with a great sense of pride and accomplishment. We thought of ourselves as the "new generation," liberated from the confines with which our parents and grandparents had lived. We felt like young rebels who were fighting the restrictions and pressing forward into a bold new world where all men were created equal.

Maybe we were overly idealistic, but most of us knew that this was the right principle by which to live. We started student committees and even won the right to dress and wear our hair as we wanted. We felt that we had the right to stand up for ourselves and fight for what we believed. We began to take an interest in politics and "rights."

On my paper route lived a girl named Linda. She was the head majorette at our school, and every day after school she and a few other girls would be outside in formation twirling their batons. My friends always wanted to ride their bikes with me and help me deliver the evening newspaper, but lost interest once we had delivered to

Linda's house. One day, Linda waved at me, and I stopped to talk to her. She was a couple of grades ahead of me, and I was surprised she even spoke to me.

"Have you heard the Beatles yet?" she asked.

I listened intently, thinking that some sort of beetle was making a cricket-like noise. "I don't hear anything," I answered.

"No, stupid! The singing group, The Beatles!" she said. "Come inside with me."

"Won't your parents be mad that you brought a guy to the house while they were at work?" I asked.

"No, my parents are cool."

We went inside. Linda took a small single record out of her pink "record case" and put it on her Hi-Fi.

The song, "She Loves You," came on. I had never heard music like that before. We listened to it over and over. I was so mesmerized I didn't even pay any attention to Linda.

When I got home that night, I called all of my friends and said, "Wait until you hear this new singing group from London! Linda let me come into her house and listen to it. It's the grooviest thing you've ever heard."

"You were listening to music in Linda's house? Yeah, right!"

"It's true," I said.

"Yeah, right!"

They were more interested in how I had gotten into Linda's house than in the Beatles.

That group took over the music world, and the whole world changed. Hippies were doing psychedelic drugs and putting flowers into the barrels of police officers' guns. We were told to make love, not war.

Skinny model Twiggy hit the runways of London and became the darling of the fashion world. I used to tear pages out of fashion magazines and use the photos of models to style my school friends' hair. I seemed to have a knack for dramatically changing someone's appearance. I had decided that my friends and I needed to have distinct "looks"—something new and fresh that would set us apart.

I was the self-appointed guru who was going to give that look to them. I painted the faces of my female friends the same way that famed British designer Mary Quant was doing makeup in London. I cut their hair in styles that I had seen Vidal Sassoon create in the pages of Vogue. I wanted my friends to dress in fashions like Twiggy and another popular model of the day, Penelope Tree, and gave them pictures as references for shopping.

Miniskirts with bold, colorful geometric shapes were the style for the girls, and bell bottoms were "in" for the guys. "Paisley" and "Op Art" were the new words added to our vocabulary.

We looked like the "Latin Mod Squad." My friends would get $10 from their parents for a haircut and I would cut it for $5. They were happy and I was even happier because I was the one behind the makeover.

At 15 years old, I saw a coupon in the newspaper for 50 percent off the $300 fee to enroll in a cosmetology school. I saved up the $150.00 and enrolled.

Monday and Thursday nights, as well as all day Saturdays, I was in "beauty school." The people who ran the school saw the natural talent and potential I had right away and immediately put me out on the "floor," doing one client after another. I learned nothing from them, but I got a lot of practice. I was the object of pride of all my instructors.

I always thanked them for all that I was "learning." As long as I made them feel worthwhile and appreciated, they let me work and create as I wanted. And I certainly needed practice to perfect my skills.

When I turned 16, I quit high school and attended the beauty school full time, working evenings as a busboy in a restaurant. Eventually, I earned the credit hours needed to graduate and get licensed. I also made tips from each client on whom I worked.

Between tips and cutting my friends' hair, I not only had money in my pocket, but I also began to save for my dream—a move to New York City.

There seemed to be only one setback that had the potential to hold back the realization of my dream. I had fallen in love with Terri, the most beautiful girl I had ever seen in person. She was over-the-top—fake eyelashes, top and bottom, too much makeup, and lots of tussled light blonde hair. She wore miniskirts and high white shiny boots. I knew the moment I first saw her that I was going to marry her.

My dream of living and working in New York finally did become a reality in 1967. I had $300 in one hand and a plane ticket in the other. I promised my future bride, that as soon as I got a job and an apartment, I would send for her and we would be married. She reminded me that I had better hurry because soon she would begin to "show." Yes, she was pregnant and the baby was mine.

So, at the age of 17, I arrived in New York City and the same day, with the help of a friend's uncle, got an apartment in the Flatbush section of Brooklyn.

The following day, I walked into the prestigious Bergdorf Goodman Beauty Salon at 5th Avenue and 57th Street in Manhattan and got a job. Although I was only an assistant, I was the youngest hairdresser ever employed at the Bergdorf Goodman Salon at the time.

Within a couple of months I was settled and I walked down the aisle in a church on 5th Avenue just a few blocks from the Metropolitan Museum of Art. My very beautiful and very pregnant bride was wearing a white lace mini wedding dress. Her mother and my father were in attendance.

CHAPTER 3

Early Success

"What does a man gain from all his labor at
which he toils under the sun?"
ECCLESIASTES 1:3

My job at Bergdorf Goodman Salon started off humbly enough, even though my attitude was a little too cocky and self-assured.

The salon manager who interviewed me was a very proper old-world diva by the name of Helen Lanier. Everyone pronounced her name Lawn-yea. That day I learned a new word — pretentious.

Miss Lanier was dressed impeccably in a dark designer suit and sat very upright. She extended her hand to me in a gesture that suggested she wanted me to kiss it rather than shake it, and she waved me to sit down.

Her eyes scanned me from head to toe. Then she spoke. "You're very young. Why do you want to work at Bergdorf's?"

"Because this is the best salon in New York and I only want to work for the best," I answered.

"What makes you think that your work is good enough for Bergdorf's?"

"My work is good enough for *anywhere*," I boasted. "Hire me, and you'll never be sorry!"

She sat staring at me, and I held her gaze. Her eyes were smiling even though she was trying hard to maintain her stern composure. I sensed that I had won her over, and that the job was mine.

"If I hired you, when could you start?" she asked.

"Right now," I answered.

"Well, I will give this serious consideration and will call you."

"Fine, but don't take too long. I might be snatched up by your competitor, and you'll never forgive yourself," I retorted, rather cockily.

She smiled without restraint and almost laughed out loud. "You're a very confident young man," she replied.

Two days later, I started as an assistant to the colorist. Not the job I wanted, but at least I got my foot in the door. Later, I was told that I was the youngest person ever hired in that salon.

Life seemed to be going well.

However, one day I arrived home from work to find Terri lying in bed. Her ankles and wrists were swollen three times their normal size. She was paler than anyone I had ever seen. Tears were running down her face, and as I lifted her head off the pillow and onto my lap, she was too weak to push air from her lungs to speak. She seemed to be drifting in and out of consciousness.

I called an ambulance and she was rushed to Brooklyn's Kings County Hospital. Doctors were speaking to me, but I couldn't understand them. Something about Terri's blood type and mine being like poison together.

They tried to induce her labor, but 36 hours later, she still couldn't deliver. A doctor met me in the waiting room and informed me that the baby was dead. It was half out of her body, but she had gone into some sort of seizure and the baby was stuck. My wife was barely clinging to life, and there was a possibility that she wouldn't make it.

My mind reeled. What would I do? How does one handle this kind of stuff? Part of me felt like a grown-up, and the other part like a little nine-year-old boy. Again, a woman I loved was sick, would die, and leave me. I felt like I couldn't handle another death.

Women were weak. Women were like flowers—beautiful to look at, but very fragile. If you pick one and take it home, it ends up dying.

Terri didn't die, but our life was never the same after that. She blamed herself for the baby's death. I blamed her for being a woman and being weak.

I had decided that she had become a burden to me, and I wouldn't let anybody hold me back from achieving my dreams. Within a short time, we had an uncontested divorce.

I was still in my teens and already divorced, but I was free to pursue all that life had to offer. It became one big party.

New York was my kind of town, right from the beginning. My future looked bright and I was full of the confidence that comes with youth. All things were possible, and I was going for the big time. No more little-town blues for me.

But, for all determination and my "wannabe" sophistication, there were many situations that reminded me of my roots.

One of these was the time Rita Hayworth walked into Bergdorf's.

Whenever a big celebrity came in, the buzz would go around among all the employees. Within minutes, everyone knew who was in the store.

One day, one of the girls on my floor came running in and said to me, "Rita Hayworth is on the first floor!"

I got so excited — a real-life movie star!

"I'll be right back. I have to see Rita Hayworth!" I said to the client whose hair I was cutting. I didn't wait for a response, as I quickly put my scissors down and ran to the elevator. I got to the first floor and the employees were all looking in one direction.

I guess I expected to see Ms. Hayworth as she had been in the movie "Gilda" — long, curly red hair that she would toss back with a flick of her head.

When I finally saw her, she looked like an old woman dressed in an elegant brown suit with a fox fur thrown over her shoulder. She was also wearing a hat cocked to one side. She looked like every other rich old lady who shopped at Bergdorf's. She probably wasn't that old, but I was only 17 at the time. Anyone over 35 was old to me. I was a little disappointed and went back upstairs to finish my haircut.

The client on whom I had been working was still sitting there, flipping through a magazine. She asked me what I thought about Rita Hayworth.

"She was just an old lady. She looked like everyone else who shops here," I said.

She laughed, and I continued to cut her hair. About 10 minutes later, Rita Hayworth herself walked into the salon.

"There she is! That's Rita Hayworth!" I said to my client.

Ms. Hayworth walked right up to us and said to my client, "Yasmin, how much longer do think you will be?"

At that moment, I wanted the earth to open up and swallow me. My client was the Princess Yasmin Aga Khan, Rita Hayworth's daughter with the Prince Aly Aga Kahn, and I didn't even know it.

"I'm not sure, Mother. Ask Danny, who's cutting my hair."

She looked at me in the mirror, and I saw a little smirk that almost made me burst out laughing. She must have gotten such a kick out of this whole thing.

Then there was the new client who sat in my chair for a haircut. She was a beautiful redheaded lawyer and, as I was cutting her hair, I began to make small talk.

"So, are you married?" I asked.

"Sort of," she answered.

Feeling very avant-garde and trendy, I said, "Oh, do you live with your boyfriend?"

"No, with my girlfriend, Danny," she answered. "I'm a lesbian."

Suddenly, my ears began to buzz, my vision closed in on me, and I fainted. That's right! I fell right to the floor.

No one had ever said anything like that to me before, and I just didn't know how to handle it. Talk about being naive! I had never met a lesbian before. When you don't know what to do or say, just faint!

Another time I was given a new client who had just walked into the salon. She wanted her hair permed and had no one particular hairdresser in mind. That's how a new hairdresser builds up a clientele.

This woman was very sweet and the first thing I did was give her a release form to fill out. A lot of salons used to do this to protect themselves against liabilities in case of a problem when doing chemical work.

After she signed the release, I brushed through her hair, being careful not to brush her scalp, the way I had been taught to do. The texture of her hair seemed dry and slightly damaged. I asked her if this was her natural color. She said, "Yes." I wet her hair and began to roll it on the perm rods.

Once I completed setting her hair, I moved her over to the sink area and applied the perm solution to each rod. My assistant, Bella, began to clean up, while I chatted with my new client.

All of a sudden, I noticed that there were heat waves coming up from her head. They looked like the heat waves that came off the road on a super-hot, dry day.

I panicked, immediately lay my client back into the sink, and turned on the water to get the solution off of her head. As the pressure of the water hose hit the rollers, they began to drop off into the sink with the hair still on them.

I looked up at Bella and her eyes were the size of half dollars. My knees started shaking. I said to Bella, "Go get Miss Lanier."

Bella darted out of the shampoo room. My client knew something had gone very wrong. She reached up and felt the places where the rollers had been. Most of them were now in the sink. She started to scream. I kept rinsing.

Miss Lanier came running into the shampoo room. My client was now crying hysterically. Miss Lanier tried to calm her.

The salon was all in a buzz. All the other hairdressers came by and poked their heads into the shampoo area. We put a towel over my client's head and were told to go into Miss Lanier's office.

"What perm solution did you use?" Miss Lanier asked.

"I used one for normal hair," I answered. "I asked her if this was her natural color and she said yes."

That's when my client spoke up. She told us that she had bleached her hair platinum blonde herself and had done such a bad job of it that she immediately colored it back to her "natural color." She said she was too embarrassed to tell me that.

We all looked at her in disbelief. My client sobbed and began to apologize to me. She actually apologized to *me* for burning all of her hair off.

Miss Lanier was a trooper and came through at that moment. She hugged the woman and said, "Don't cry, dear. Let's see what we can do about this mishap. We're going to help you."

She immediately called in the wig maker who worked in the salon, and we measured the client's head for a wig.

"What kind of style do you want the wig to be made in?" the wig maker asked.

That's when I piped up and said, "Let's make the wig in a very modern style, like the ones we see in the magazines. Let's do it in a short Vidal Sassoon haircut like Mia Farrow's. That way, as your hair grows out, we can begin to trim it to look like the wig, and no one will ever know when it goes from your wig to your hair."

We all agreed that this was a good idea. We also said we would provide her with free conditioners and haircuts for a year.

Then, Miss Lanier picked up her phone and called downstairs to the women's accessories department and asked the salesgirl to bring up a couple of dozen head turbans in a variety of colors and patterns.

As the months went by, my client's hair grew into a really cute pixie-like haircut. By then, I had convinced her that this was the best thing that could have happened to her. I told her that she was the most modern looking woman who came to the Bergdorf's salon. The funny thing is—I really meant it.

Miss Lanier seemed to like me, even though I did screw things up now and then. One day we got a call from someone who was putting together an award show. The presenter of the show was going to be Ginger Rogers. A hairdresser was needed to help Ms. Rogers with her hair. She was an old lady by then, but to me she was still a movie star.

I got picked to take the day off from the salon and help her. I was like a little boy counting the days until Christmas, as I waited for the "big" day to come. That day I woke up extra early and jumped on the subway from Brooklyn to Manhattan with great anticipation. Maybe this was the big break I needed.

I arrived at the theater where the event was being held and filmed. I set up all my equipment in the dressing room and waited for Ms. Rogers to show up.

When she finally appeared, she was wearing a large "poncho," her head was wrapped in a turban, and she had on very large sunglasses. She really did look like a movie star.

Once in the dressing room, we were introduced. I wanted to tell her what a big fan I have been since I was a little boy, but thought better about it. That kind of compliment is a double-edged sword—it might please her, but it might also remind her that she was a movie star long before I was born and make her feel old. I said nothing.

After Ms. Rogers removed the poncho, turban, and sunglasses, I realized that I didn't have to say anything to make her feel old. She *was* old. As a matter of fact, she could have been any old lady walking down the street. She could have been my grandmother.

There was nothing about her that said "Ginger Rogers" except that fantastically well-shaped body that screamed "dancer."

I set her hair with hot rollers and started to work on a hairpiece that would add volume to her now thin hair. I watched in fascination as she transformed herself with makeup.

She had makeup tricks that I had never seen before. For one, she covered her entire eyelid with eyelash glue. Next, she pulled out a toothpick, laid it on her eyelid, and rolled up all the excess skin. Then with one finger holding the lid in place, she slipped the toothpick out.

When she saw me watching in utter amazement, she commented that the glue also helped the eye shadow stay on all day. We both laughed. She then proceeded to literally paint Ginger Rogers onto her face. Her lips were painted in the shape of Ginger's "movie" lips, totally disregarding the outline of her own lips.

After I got her hair "on," there she was in all her former glory— Ginger Rogers—or the illusion of Ginger Rogers.

I loved my job. I had been training for it all my life.

I stepped out of the dressing room so that Ms Rogers could get dressed. Her wardrobe girl had finished steaming all of her clothes.

When the door opened again, out stepped Ginger in a floor-length red sequined gown that was skin-tight. A red-feathered boa was draped over her shoulders. She was a transvestite's dream.

Someone mentioned that she was probably wearing a full body suit, because no one that age could have a body like that.

I looked around at all the photographers and spotted one from the Associated Press whom I knew. I walked over to him and said, "Hey, Bob! If I can get Ginger to give you two minutes for solo pictures, would you take a picture of her and me together?"

"You bet!" he answered.

Then I walked over to Ginger and asked her if it was okay to take a picture with her. We had gotten along so well in the dressing room that she didn't hesitate to agree.

We stepped over to an area where Bob could photograph us. As I stood beside her, I decided to find out for myself whether she was wearing a body suit under that dress or not.

I put my arm around her just under her armpit, let my hand slide down her body to her hip, and smiled for the camera.

Ginger turned to me with a sly smile, "Not bad, huh?"

"What?" I answered, playing stupid.

"The feel you just got," she said.

I don't think I had ever blushed before in my life, but suddenly my face burned. I sensed that it had turned bright red. Even my eyeballs burned.

Ginger laughed out loud, leaned over, and kissed me on the cheek. Just at that moment, Bob snapped the greatest picture. I cherished it for years.

By the way, not only was there no body suit, but there was nothing under that dress but Ginger.

Another time, I was sent out on an assignment for *Seventeen Magazine*. They wanted someone young to come to the studio and do hair that was appropriate for hip young girls who were being photographed for a spread on "The New Generation."

I was 17 years old, so it only seemed right to send me. I was excited when I got to the studio. The fashion editor asked if I had ever been in a photo studio before.

"Are you kidding? I grew up in a photo studio. My dad is a photographer," I answered.

One of the models was actually a client of mine at Bergdorf's. Maybe she was the one who had recommended me.

I blow-dried those models' hair as straight as I could. Then I decided that I wanted their hair even straighter.

I asked the wardrobe girl for an ironing board and an iron to be brought to me. I laid the girls' heads back on the board and brushed it flat down. Then I tore a paper bag in half, laid it over the hair, and ironed on the paper bag. Now the hair was dead, dead straight. No one had ever seen this before. Remember, there were no flat irons back then. This was how I used to iron my stepmother's hair when I was younger. It was a hit.

When the pictures came out, for the first time ever I saw my name in print. The credit read: "Hair by Danny Velasco for Bergdorf Goodman Beauty Salon."

No one was doing hair or makeup for editorial work in magazines back then. I decided that I was going to devote part of my time to this kind of work and get my name in the magazines as often as possible. I didn't realize back then that one day I would work exclusively on photo shoots.

After working at Bergdorf's for a couple of years, it seemed to me that they were stuck in another era. I no longer felt that it was the best salon in New York. In fact, I thought they were dated and behind the times.

One day I marched into the office of my salon manager and told her even though Bergdorf's thought Jackie Kennedy Onassis was the fashion icon of the whole world that was not the case.

Times had changed. Young people were not happy coming to the same beauty salons that their Mothers went to, and they did not want to look like Jackie. Bergdorf's was old-fashioned. I had expected the best salon in the world to be more cutting edge than that.

Miss Lanier smiled when I told her that, asked me to close the door, and take a seat. She then proceeded to tell me that the corporate office was already aware of the problem.

Corporate Office—what did that mean?

That's when I found out that the beauty salon at Bergdorf Goodman was a leased space owned by a large chain of salons by the name of the Glemby Company.

"Very soon, we are going to open a small haircutting and blow-drying salon on the Junior Floor of Bergdorf's—for the young clients," she informed me. "These clients will never have to come to their mothers' salon again. You will be trained and you will be working downstairs on the 5th floor with three other young people who will be hired. We are going to advertise it, promote it, and we want it to be the new trendy place for young people to get their hair done."

I can't tell you how excited I was. I was not going to be a mere assistant any more. I was going to do the kind of work that I had been doing for years already. My practice models had been my family and my friends. I was ready to take on New York City.

Right from the start, this small salon located on Bergdorf's Junior Floor was taking in 10 times the amount of money that the main salon was. This was measured by per-square-foot of leased space.

When the doors of Bergdorf's would open, the young girls would rush in and run up to the 5th floor. You would have thought it was a rock concert.

Glemby's profits began to soar and a decision was made to install these small salon units in department stores across the country. They already had the space leased. These newly opened places would do nothing but haircutting and blow-drying. On top of that, they wanted me to stop working in the salon and work instead with a small team that would train the 17,000 hairdressers they employed.

Within a year, the Glemby Corporate Training Program was in full swing. A British couple called the Chadwicks were brought to America and put in charge of the program. I was second in command, along with two of my friends.

I was earning a fortune compared to what I had been making before. I was given an expense account that allowed for couture designer clothes, dinners in the best restaurants, as well as for entertaining and limousines. Our bosses wanted us to personify the company—young, successful, and loyal to the Glemby name.

Part of the job also called for us to be responsible for all the large poster-sized photos that you see in most beauty salons. We had to produce different pictures for each salon group, and that meant dozens of photos each season.

After several photo shoots, we realized that something was wrong with the way we did this. We would hire a top makeup artist to do the makeup and a top wardrobe stylist to go to the designers' showrooms and choose the clothes. Then we would hire a photographer who came with assistants, for which we also had to pay.

Models are expensive and we needed lots of them. On the actual day of the photo shoot, we would all be together. Only one or two of us could do hair at the same time, so eight of us would stand around like dummies saying dumb hairdresser things like "Gorgeous!" "Fabulous!" "Awesome!"

In order to save money on our budget with these photo shoots, we decided that each of us would take over a different aspect of the operation. My friend Louis was chosen to make the contacts at the designer showrooms. John would take the pictures and his wife Susie would do hair. I was chosen to learn makeup, since I always loved painting. All the others were to assist in any way they could.

We hired our friends as models, along with any cute girl we happened to meet on the street or in a club. They were happy to make two or three hundred dollars, and we saved a bundle. The plan worked and I also rediscovered a long lost talent—makeup!

I say "long lost" because I think back to the days when I practiced on my little stepsisters. I used to torture them by painting them up like little hussies, chopping their hair off, and gluing their eyelids together trying to stick false eyelashes on them. Hey, practice makes perfect, right?

Next, for me, was Europe. At the age of 21 years old, I took over the London training operations of the Glemby Company. I was given a residence in the posh Paddington section of Westminster that came complete with a full-time housekeeper.

I opened and ran a school for advanced hairdressing for all European employees. I loved the way the young people on London's Carnaby Street dressed, so I emulated them by wearing giant bell-bottoms with platform shoes that were made to order.

Flying to Paris or Amsterdam for the weekend became a frequent thing to do. Sometimes, I would fly to Paris for the day just to buy shoes. I was making friends all over the world and I loved it.

On my trips back to New York, we would work out of a facility on Madison Avenue where we designed programs to teach masses of hairdressers the most popular haircuts and trends. We broke our techniques down into a step-by-step process, with guidelines so detailed that we could have taught a gorilla to do beautiful hair.

Our team promoted the schools both in the United States and in Europe with demonstrations for thousands of hairdressers at hairdressing conventions. These conventions would fill auditoriums such as the Royal Albert Hall in London and many venues all over the United States and Mexico.

My ego was out of control. But something else began to brew—the panic attacks started. I found it strange I could speak to an audience of 10,000 people and not be intimidated, but standing in line at the grocery store could bring on such anxiety that the closer I got to the cash register, the harder it would be to breathe. I once left a cart full of groceries in the line and ran out of the store thinking I would suffocate if I didn't get outside fast enough.

A doctor prescribed Valium for the panic attacks, and I quickly found out that Valium worked much better when washed down with vodka. I started to drink heavily and always had the Valium on me. This opened a door to almost 20 years of drug abuse that would progressively get worse and worse.

I had managed to get through the 1960s without using drugs, but the 1970s were a different story. I was in my early 20s and I began to use drugs with abandon. Having all the money I needed, I would have dealers come to my apartment with backpacks full of drugs. It was like a personal drug shopping spree. I could have my choice of any drug I wanted—pot, hashish, cocaine, whatever. The line between partying and business had also blurred.

Studio 54, the legendary Manhattan disco, was my favorite hangout for both.

Everyone with whom I had contact loved the glitz and glamour of Studio 54, and I was in the middle of it all. Almost every night of the week when I was in New York, I ended up at Studio 54.

It was where I partied and entertained people, and where I could let loose and do anything I wanted to do. It was like a neutral zone, where people from every walk of life would come together and rub shoulders with gangsters or world-famous personalities. If you were cool enough to always be let in, you were cool enough to party with.

I remember seeing Diana Ross sitting on O.J. Simpson's shoulders, singing together her hit, "Baby Love," as everyone cheered. I also remember Bianca Jagger coming into the club and right out onto the dance floor on a large white stallion.

You could be on the dance floor dancing next to Cher or fashion designer Halston, as Calvin Klein leaned against the bar in a white tee shirt and Levis. Some of the most beautiful and bizarre people in the world were there and got away with any way they wanted to present themselves.

One of them was an eccentric looking woman who wore only a floor-length wedding veil, white garter belt, white nylons, and white high heels—nothing else except her makeup and perfume. Then, there was the 90-year-old woman with a fancy for beautiful young topless studs who sat at her feet as she held court on a settee. There were the pre-Goth punk rockers, dressed like the corpses on their way to a funeral. It was a visual spectacle each and every night of the week.

All too often, I went overboard. Once, I woke up to someone hitting me with a broom. The lights of Studio 54 were all on. The nightclub was empty and the cleaning crew had found me passed out, lying behind a sofa.

My job with Glemby was beginning to bore me. I wanted to work with famous models and celebrities, but I felt that I was stuck in a corporate merry-go-round, being merely the liaison between 17,000 hairdressers and corporate headquarters.

So, at the age of 27, after a decade of working for other people, I decided to take my chances and start a career as a freelance hairdresser and makeup artist.

I quit my job with Glemby and set out to make my own history.

CHAPTER 4

Early Addiction

"I denied myself nothing my eyes desired; I
refused my heart no pleasure."
ECCLESIASTES 2:10A

The year was 1979. I was 29 years old and in trouble. Work was coming in slowly, and not the kind for which I'd hoped. I had expected to be further along on my new career path by then. The jobs for which I was getting paid well were not what I wanted. Wiping mayonnaise off a kid's face for TV commercials was not my idea of a career in fashion.

I needed an agent, someone to represent me and find me work. I wanted to work on the "real" fashion scene—do hair and makeup for the leading fashion magazines such as *Vogue, Bazaar, Cosmopolitan,* and *Glamour.* These were the "Bibles" of the fashion world. I wanted to create beautiful images, and I wanted everyone to know who did it.

In the midst of my frustration, I had one small glimmer of hope. I had done a photo shoot with a young model named Carol Alt, which had ended up on the cover of *Harper's Bazaar.* That was when I was introduced to a young woman named Toni.

Toni had beautiful, long, curly blonde hair and a million-dollar smile. She had grown up in Long Island, NY, and was a bubbly and bright woman who could talk about anything and everything.

She told me that she had always wanted to be an agent and be involved in the fashion industry. She knew all about every fashion designer and could comment on all the collections. She told me she would represent me as her only client and later build her business from *there.* She seemed excited by the whole idea, and I felt that she would be a good person to represent me.

She also turned me on to the best drugs I ever had. I ended up going home with her to a beautiful apartment on Park Avenue every night, and she would order food to be delivered from the best restaurants in New York.

"How do you get the Waldorf Astoria to deliver lobster here?" I asked.

"All it takes is money," she answered.

Toni was flippant and alive, and her eyes sparkled. At times, she looked so beautiful I couldn't keep my eyes off her. Lobster, Cristal Champagne, chocolate mousse, and then the drugs would come out. Toni knew what I wanted and lavishly furnished it. She seemed to have a never-ending supply of money. If I ever wondered where it came from, I never asked.

She set up one of the rooms in her apartment as an office. She had phone and fax lines put in and ordered stationery and cards to establish the new business. The trouble was that no work ever came in because Toni did very little to get me clients.

Money for me was very tight. I was no longer able to continue to pay the rent on my huge loft. It didn't take Toni long to talk me into giving up my place and moving in with her. I didn't know at the time that Toni was a control freak, but it would soon become painfully clear.

Drugs were always available, but dispensed by Toni. I had no access to the locked walk-in closet where the supplies were kept, and I was never given keys to the apartment either. She began to control my every move. If I received or made a phone call, she wanted to know to whom I was talking and about what. When I would leave the apartment, there were always a thousand questions and lots of slamming of things, followed by the "cold shoulder" treatment.

Eventually, she wore me down and I went along with it to keep the peace. I knew that going against Toni's wishes or opposing any of her whims wasn't a good idea. She wanted things her way, and she was a force with which to reckon. Days and nights began to mean nothing anymore. I slept whenever I wanted and woke up whenever I wanted. Most times, I wasn't even aware of what day of the week it was.

Toni was reclusive, so I became a recluse too. She felt secure and in control of her own environment and didn't like to venture out too much where she felt she wasn't in control of things and of me.

I rarely touched money. Toni took care of everything. I never left the apartment without her. When we would go out to dinner or to another event, a limousine would pick us up at the entrance of her building and take us wherever she wanted to go. Our most frequent outings were to pick up money and deliver drugs.

By this time, I knew that Toni was not just a bubbly, charming woman with the face of an angel. She was also a high-powered drug dealer who organized drug runs from India to the United States and was making money hand over fist.

For the next year and a half, I was her captive, controlled by her drugs and money. My life had been reduced to this. Day after day, I struggled with myself. I beat myself up for being so weak that I couldn't just walk away. My family couldn't stand the fact that I was kept away from them. They thought I had come under some kind of a spell, and, in a way, I had.

I felt helpless and hopeless. What would I do? Where would I go? I began to make secret plans to escape. I started to hide money here and there. Sometimes, it was just three or four dollars, other times 10 or 20. But even if I could get enough money together, how would I leave? I knew I couldn't stand up to Toni.

From a self-assured, cocky, and "well-to-do" teen who had plenty of money to throw around, I was reduced to a pauper desperately hatching an escape plan.

I finally got to the point where I couldn't take this kind of life anymore. I had managed to accumulate $1,000 from all the secretly collected change, and I had hidden this money all over the apartment in case one of the stashes was found.

One night, while Toni slept, I dressed in the dark, put some clothes she had bought me in a small bag, grabbed my hairdressing and makeup equipment that I hadn't even looked at in months, and quietly let myself out of the apartment.

Once downstairs, I jumped into a taxi and went to JFK airport. I bought a ticket on the next flight to Paris and waited to board the plane. With me, I had my one cover of *Bazaar* magazine. It was the job I had done for free and *Bazaar* had decided to publish it. I carried the magazine with me in a manila envelope. I also had the names of several contacts in Paris that I had collected from various people. I was desperate. Paris was far away from New York and Toni. If I was going to revive my career (or my life, for that matter), Paris would be the best place to go.

A new start, a new life—that was all I thought about as I boarded that plane.

Part of me felt elated to be free at last, and another part was terrified. But I knew that whatever came my way had to be better than the life I had now. Though I had hoped to put the past months of my life behind me, the Toni saga didn't quite end there.

I arrived at Charles de Gaulle airport early the next morning. I went straight to a phone and called one of the contact names I had with me. Her name was Janet and that was all I knew about her, but I was assured by the person who gave me her number that she was sweet and loved visitors from the States. I was not disappointed.

I told her on the phone that I had just arrived in Paris and had no idea where to even begin to look for a place to stay. She gave me her address, told me to come right over, and she would help me. Given my track record with Toni, it is unbelievable now—as I look back on it—that I fell into the "come stay with me" ploy again.

I arrived at a lovely building on the Left Bank and rang Janet's bell. By her voice on the phone, I had assumed that she was British and was very surprised when a young Chinese woman opened the door.

As we began to talk over coffee and crêpes (thin French pancakes), I found out that her parents were Chinese, but she was born and raised in New Zealand. As a young hippie, she had set out with a backpack to see the world.

Arriving in Paris, she had taken a job as an au-pair (nanny) to a divorced man with two children. She alluded to him having been someone of noble birth. His family lived in exile in Paris. As a matter of fact, the family owned the entire building. Aunts, uncles, and cousins occupied every apartment.

Janet had fallen in love with her employer and they had married. Now, besides the two children he'd had with another wife, they had a child of their own. I was fascinated. *The Nanny* wasn't even a TV series yet, but someone who knew this couple could have written it.

"How long will you be staying in Paris?" Janet asked. "And where have you thought of staying?"

"Indefinitely, and I have no idea where to even look for a room," I answered.

"Then why not just stay here?" she said. "We have an empty maid's suite just across the hall. It has a small living room and a bedroom. You can stay there until you start working and earning money, and then you can find a place of your own."

I moved right in.

Two days later, I was calling every magazine in the phone book, asking to meet with any fashion or beauty editor who would give me an appointment. It was a good thing that I had learned French while working at Bergdorf's, so I was fluent.

I bought a map of Paris, and with Janet's help I rode the metro and went from one appointment to another. Maybe I should say from one disappointment to another.

Every editor I met asked me the same question, "Can I see your portfolio of work?"

All I had was a manila envelope with one picture in it—my *Bazaar* cover of model Carol Alt. The editors looked at me in disbelief.

"How can I show you what I can do if you won't hire me to work for your magazine?" I asked, again and again.

I tried my charm, but these were hard-core editors who had seen portfolios of work by the best hairdressers and makeup artists in the world. I was a joke, and I knew it. It was hard to keep up the confident front.

I felt depressed and destined to go back to Toni and beg for forgiveness, but another part of me would rather jump in the Seine River than to go back to that life.

At the end of my first day of "go sees," I felt defeated and discouraged. Still, I headed to the last appointment of the day, with a fashion stylist whose name I had brought with me from New York.

I arrived at her apartment and rang the bell. When she opened the door, she took one look at me and said, "You look like you could use a drink."

"A large vodka, please," I replied.

She proceeded to pour me a large glass of vodka on ice and I plopped down on her sofa. "I'm at a loss," I told her. "I'm really talented and I want to work, but I can't get anyone to give me a break. I have no portfolio, just one picture in a manila envelope."

"Let's see your one picture in a manila envelope," she said, sounding amused.

I handed her my envelope and she pulled out my only piece of work.

"It's lovely!" she exclaimed.

"Yeah, but it's nothing compared to what I can do. Do you think you can give me the names of some photographers that might let me work? I'll even work for free. I would work for free just to show them what I'm capable of."

Yes, I was that desperate.

"I think I can help," she said. "I'll see what I can do."

The vodka was starting to do its magic and I began to relax. We talked for what seemed like hours. She was smart and seemed to know everyone and everything about the fashion business.

I left her apartment late that night and headed back to my small rooms on the Left Bank to lick my wounds.

The next afternoon, I was awakened by Janet, who seemed very excited and couldn't wait any longer for me to wake up on my own.

"Italian *Vogue* magazine called and wants you to work next week," she said excitedly. "They want you to call them today. You've got to call right away!"

I jumped out of bed and got right on the phone.

"Thank you for calling, Danny. Hannah Fox wants to book you for next Monday. Are you available?" said the voice on the other side of the phone.

Was she kidding? I was available for the rest of my life!

"Hannah Fox, the stylist I met last night? Tell her I will be wherever she wants me to go at whatever time she wants me there!" I responded.

"Good, be at Pin-up Studio at 7AM Monday morning. And, Danny, Hannah is not a stylist. She's our Fashion and Beauty Editor. See you Monday."

Fashion and Beauty Editor? I was blown away. I had been given a break. I was going to do the best job ever. Only one day, but I was going to give it my all.

On Monday morning, I arrived at the studio bright and early. Hannah came in and barely looked at me but managed to give me a little wink and a nod.

The first model arrived, and I was ready for her. I wanted to do something different, something that I had never seen in a fashion magazine before. I didn't want to copy anyone else's work.

When I had finished getting the model ready, Hannah took one look at her, turned to me, and said, "Consider yourself booked for the rest of the week. I wanted to see your work in person before committing to the entire week. Now that I've seen it, I want you to stay."

Then I saw Hanna go to work dressing the model. That's when I understood why she was in her position. She was amazing as she began to create a fantasy in white toile, silk organza, and diamonds. The gown was already there, but everything that went with it was Hannah's creation. I stood back in genuine admiration for her talent. I was happy to be working with her.

Then the photographer did the most beautiful lighting on the model's face, which made whatever I had done look 10 times better.

Finally, we were ready to shoot, and the photographer took time to crop the picture in a tight frame close-up. The model went into a pose that made her look strong yet vulnerable at the same time. The photographer let us all look into the lens of the camera, and it was like looking at a vision. It was everything I had ever dreamed of. I was working with a team of super-talented people. It made me want to create and spurred me on to be better than I ever thought I could be. That old feeling of excitement flooded over me once again. It was like a high and I was getting the drug my ego needed. I was full of dreams of greatness and fame again.

This spur-of-the-moment escape to Paris had been a good move after all. I was going to make it big time. By the end of the week, we had not only shot enough photos that could be used for several issues, but also cover tries. Each magazine shoots several different versions of the cover and only chooses one each month.

Even if I didn't get the cover, I had a shot at it, and most of the other photos would definitely make it into the pages of the magazine.

Hannah had also recommended me to a friend of hers who was an editor at German *Vogue* magazine. They had booked me for a trip the following two weeks to Sri Lanka. From there, I was to fly to Portugal for another 10 days.

Altogether, it was enough work for five months' worth of issues of the magazines. I was also told that I should find an agent in Paris as quickly as possible, because when all this work hit the newsstands, my career would go through the roof.

Those words we like music to my ears.

Several weeks later, I returned from all of these trips and as I was walking through the Paris airport, there on the newsstand was my first European cover of *Vogue*.

I could hardly contain my excitement. I bought every issue I could find at that airport. I thought that if I couldn't carry my bags and the magazines at the same time, I would leave my bags and take just the magazines. I had my priorities straight!

At last, my dreams were coming true and the money began to roll in. I found an agent, a beautiful apartment with a view of the Eiffel Tower, and I started to explore my new city.

Paris was home now. It was far from my old life and far from Toni. But I knew that Toni read all the European fashion magazines, and it took her no time to find me.

She called on the day my new phone was installed. Somehow she had gotten the number. When I heard her bubbly, "Hi!", a cold chill ran through my body. She spoke to me as if nothing had ever happened. She told me how thrilled she was to see my work in the magazines. She said she couldn't wait for me to come home so that we could get to work in New York. I was so shocked, I couldn't say a word. I felt as if I were frozen in some suspended time warp.

There was no mention of my escape while she slept. It was scary, because so many months had passed. I had been away from her long enough now to realize how completely delusional she was.

I was being stalked by a crazy woman. I was afraid of her and of what she might do. Was there no place I could go to that was beyond her reach?

CHAPTER 5

Renewed Success

"My heart took delight in all my work, and this
was the reward for all my labors."
ECCLESIASTES 2:10B

Photographers who wouldn't have given me the time of day before were now calling. Magazine editors who had practically laughed me out of their offices a few months earlier now asked me to come see them because they had some projects for me. I no longer had to try to find ways to meet them.

My new agent set a pretty high day fee for me to work in the studio. Other agents were calling me from all over the world.

Within a couple of months, I was calling all the shots. I now had an agent in Paris, one in Munich, one in London, and one in Milan. Agents were calling from New York, imploring me not to forget them, whenever I decided to come home for any length of time.

All the agents competed for my time. They offered me jobs, and I would choose which ones would be better for my career or for my bank account. Some jobs offered exposure to good clients and good photographers, and they were good for my future in the business. Other jobs were great for the money that the clients were willing to pay, but I wouldn't necessarily want people to know I did them because they were not considered prestigious enough.

Fortunately for me, some of the opportunities that came my way had it all—good photographer, great client, terrific exposure, and fabulous money.

I felt in control. I could say yes or no to whatever I wanted. Sometimes, I had several choices and all were good. At other times, when I couldn't accept a job because I was working on another project, I became even more in demand.

It was all a game and I was a willing player.

I realized that in order to be the first to do something different in this cut-throat editorial world, I couldn't look at what others were already doing with hair or makeup. I had to set my own style.

Our natural tendency is to look through the magazines, see something we like, and copy it to some degree. But I knew whatever was shown in a magazine had been created two or three months earlier. In a sense, it was already dated. I would come up with something that looked very different. For example, I would do the makeup with very black smoky eyes, no blusher, and pale beige lips. I would then copy that look or a variation thereof on every model for every magazine I worked with for two months.

Then, when the first magazine I had worked on using that particular look hit the newsstands, I would change the look completely. I knew that all the other magazines with whom I had worked would be coming out over the next two months with the same look. So I would do something totally different, like no eye makeup except mascara, a little blusher on the ball of the cheek, and dark red matte lips. I would stick with that look for two months or so.

Just when people thought that they had my style down, everything would be new. After a while, you can tell who is looking at your work and copying it. But, by the time they emulated my style, and their work came out in a magazine, it was already four months old, and I could see which makeup artists were styling themselves after me. It was a good way to stay ahead of the pack and to have people follow me, and not vice versa. Like I said, it was all a game and I was a willing player. I played to win.

I began to travel all over the world. Home base was Paris. I worked hard and played harder. I was living again in the fast lane and loving every minute of it.

The Paris "club scene" didn't interest me much. It seemed mild compared to Studio 54, but I loved the party scene in cities like Munich, Berlin, and Amsterdam. So every chance I got, I was off to Germany or Holland for the weekend.

Although I worked for all the magazines and many fashion designers, one very high profile designer in particular loved my work. Ever since I was a teenager in the 1960s, I had admired his work. His brightly colored geometric patterns on short mini shifts had sent him into super stardom back then. I had never even met the man, but he gave me the choice jobs. Let me explain what I mean by choice jobs, and it will give you a glimpse of what my days used to be like.

The fashion shows gear up in Paris. Models arrive from all over the world, going from one designer showroom to another, showing their pictures and hoping to get booked to walk the runway for as many shows as possible.

My agent would decide what shows were possible for me, and then I would choose which ones I wanted to do. When the job was booked, I would meet with the designer and see drawings of the collection. The designer would show me who his muse was. In other words, who was the woman he had in mind when he designed the collection. Maybe the muse would be tall and thin with short dark hair. Or perhaps she would have a pale face with colorful but smoky eyes, and pale, glossy lips.

I would collect this information from the designer of each show and purchase all the products needed to make sure that all the hairdressers and makeup artists who were working the show with me had the same products.

Sometimes, I could get companies to supply the hair products or makeup that we needed in return for a credit on the program. Copies of the collection drawings would be duplicated for each hairdresser and makeup artist working on the show.

The days of the actual shows were chaotic. Everybody ran around backstage getting ready. Hair and makeup would be done as quickly as possible according to the drawings we had been given, as well as the overall look of the show.

Once the show started and the first model hit the runway, she walked out as though this was all easy. As she strutted down the runway showing off her outfit, few people in the audience were aware of the craziness going on backstage.

The show seemed to be over very quickly, but, in fact, it went on for 45 minutes or so. However, as soon as it finished, everyone scurried off as fast as he or she could to get to the next show in another tent. It all started again—old makeup off, new makeup on, changed hair and attitude.

By the end of the day, all I could do was drop down on my bed and sleep for a couple of hours before the shows started again the next day. Hardcore partygoers (myself included) would stop at the latest, trendiest club on the way home and get smashed.

When the shows were over, the magazine photo shoots began. Big designers designate three or four outfits for each big-name magazine— four outfits for *Vogue,* four for *Bazaar,* two for *Cosmo,* two for *Elle,* etc.

When someone is the key hair or makeup person, he or she usually travels from one photo shoot to another with the models who were chosen by the designer to represent his or her new collection. Sometimes the models are the same for each magazine and sometimes they are different. That is the designer's decision.

Vogue usually puts their biggest paying client on the cover. That means the designer who purchases the most pages of advertising space for that month. After the shows, all the designers compete for the most pages of advertising so that their outfits will appear on the cover. I tried to always find out who that designer would be to guarantee that my work would also make the cover.

After the several weeks it took to get all the photo shooting done, I still didn't get a chance to relax because the shows were then taken to Milan, London, and New York.

Then, there were the shows that most people never heard about— the private shows. Like the ones in Saudi Arabia, done only for the seven royal families that controlled all the oil and all the money. This meant numerous wives, sisters, cousins, and other female relatives who had millions of dollars at their disposal, but couldn't leave the country by themselves to spend the money. So, the top designer shows conveniently came to them.

One year, a designer with whom I often worked and who I won't name (he is now retired, but at the time he was at the top) told me that a Saudi princess had bought his entire collection, paying hundreds of thousands of dollars for it. He asked me to fly to Abu Dhabi and make her look like the muse in his drawings. My fee was to be paid by the princess herself. I agreed to go and the arrangements were made.

When the day came, I boarded a private jet at Charles de Gaulle Airport that looked like a modern apartment inside. It had two bedrooms and a bathroom complete with a shower. The "living room" was all white, super modern and looked like something out of a 1960s sci-fi movie. I was the only passenger on board, apart from the flight crew.

When, many hours later, the plane landed in Saudi Arabia, it was met by two lines of soldiers forming a pathway from the steps of the plane to the open door of a waiting Rolls Royce.

The heat slammed me as I got off the plane. The driver took my bags, put them in the car, and asked me for my passport. He then disappeared for a few minutes. He spoke English to me, so when he got back to the car, I asked him to return my passport. He replied that it would be given back to me upon leaving the country. This made me nervous, but I tried to remain calm. I asked my driver were he had learned English and he told me that he was Egyptian by birth, but grew up in Brooklyn, NY. What a small world it was!

We rode for what seemed like a couple of hours. As far as I could see, there was nothing but desert sand all around. Then, in the distance, I spotted what looked like a small complex of garden apartments with a swimming pool and tennis courts. The driver stopped in front of one of the units. He came around and opened my door, and then opened the trunk to take out my luggage.

"This is where you will stay until the princess is ready to see you," he said.

"Okay… and when will that be?"

"Whenever she decides to see you," he answered.

I was not feeling in control here.

He opened the door to my apartment, carried my bags into the bedroom, and turned on the air conditioner. He then led me to the kitchen and opened the cabinets to show me that they were fully stocked with food, water, fresh fruit, and Coca-Cola.

Then, on his way out, he stopped at what looked like a side cabinet next to the sofa, and kicked the door of the cabinet lightly with his foot. It spun around to reveal a Lazy Susan filled with every kind of liquor one could imagine. He winked at me and walked out the door.

"I will return for you when the princess is ready to see you," he said. He got into the Rolls and drove away.

I stood in the doorway, looking out at the expanse of sand in the most oppressive heat I had ever experienced. Heat waves came off everything in sight.

I closed the door and wondered if I would ever get out of this alive. What if the princess hated her hair and makeup? Would anyone ever look for me if I didn't return? Would my government do anything? Would there be any record of me ever having been here?

Oh well, it was too late to worry now. I could only hope for the best.

CHAPTER 6

Europe and the World:
Life in the Fast Lane

*"There is a time for everything and a season for every
activity under heaven. A time to live and a time to die."*
ECCLESIASTES 3:1

The following morning, I got up, showered, and got dressed. I made some coffee and turned on the TV. The only channel in English was the BBC. I waited for the Rolls to come and take me to the princess.

I kept glancing at my watch—10 o'clock, 11 o'clock, 12 o'clock, 1 o'clock. No car, no phone calls, nothing to indicate what the plan was. Finally, I decided to take off my clothes and go swimming, but I remembered that I didn't bring a bathing suit with me. So, I decided to go swimming in my underwear.

Standing in the doorway of my apartment in my skivvies, I wondered whether going out in public in this kind of attire would be punishable by death. I shouted out the door, to no one in particular, "HELLO, ANYBODY THERE?"

There was no response. I assumed it was safe for me to venture outside. I carefully stepped out of the apartment. The heat was intense. The cement was burning my bare feet and the sand was even hotter. Hopping as fast as I could to avoid third-degree burns to the soles of my feet, I got to the pool and in I jumped.

The water was warm but refreshing. I stayed in the pool for a while and came out to sit in a lounge chair. But the sun was scorching, so I jumped into the pool again. Finally, I retreated back to the air-conditioned apartment and opened a bottle of vodka.

This went on for two more days. I thought I would go out of my mind. Every morning I would get up, shower, get dressed, and wait.

Sometime in the afternoon, I would get undressed and go for a swim. Then, back to the apartment and drink until I passed out.

Finally, on the fourth day, I heard a car and looked out the window to see the Rolls parked outside. The Egyptian driver knocked on the door. I opened it immediately.

"The princess will see you this morning," he announced.

I grabbed my hair and makeup bag and went to the car.

We drove for quite a long time and in the distance I could see what looked like a small, white-washed, walled city. We pulled up to the gates and were let in by two men dressed in white. The Rolls passed through, right into a tropical paradise.

The walls of the living quarters surrounded the magnificently landscaped tropical foliage. Beautiful flowers were everywhere. It was like an Arabian Nights fantasy, and I almost expected to see a flying carpet overhead. I was in awe. I realized how privileged I was to see things that very few people would ever see.

The car came to a stop. The driver jumped out, came around, opened my door, and grabbed my bag. He then led me to a part of the house that was huge and decorated with magnificent silks, sofas, and pillows.

A servant woman, who spoke to me in French, greeted me. She took my bag and waved me to be seated. Young women came out from another door, carrying what looked like a small table. They gave me hot, wet towels to wipe my hands and face. Then other girls came out with many silver covered dishes filled with delicacies for me to eat. I knew that I must taste every piece and comment favorably on each one. I knew all that because the driver had already prepped me on the protocol.

"Taste everything they offer you," he instructed. "It will insult them if you don't. And when you meet the princess you must not look at her face or touch her until you actually work on her."

I bowed my head as I tasted each dish and praised it. I didn't even want to know what I was eating. Don't ask, don't tell. But I can say that I had never before seen or tasted some of the dishes that were set before me.

Finally, more hot wet towels were brought and the original servant woman who spoke French came back to lead me into the inner sanctums of the princess's quarters.

I was taken to a bedroom with a large bed and an even larger mirrored vanity table that looked like something out of an old Hollywood movie. Laid out on the mirrored surface of the vanity was all my equipment, cleaned and carefully placed.

I stood and waited. Soon, a very young girl entered the room in a white terrycloth robe, with a white towel twisted up on her head. I diverted my eyes and saw only her feet as she walked by me. She sat at her vanity and her servant removed the towel from her head. Long, beautiful dark hair tumbled down past her shoulders.

The servant combed out the tangles, turned to me, and handed me the comb. I stepped forward, took the comb and, for the first time, I looked through the mirror directly at the princess's face. She was absolutely beautiful, and she was just a girl. She had to be all of 18 or 19 years old.

I smiled; she smiled back, and kind of giggled with her servant. A sketch of the designer's muse was leaning against the mirror. The drawing of the muse had very short dark hair. The Princess had her hair down past her shoulders.

I pointed to the sketch and tried to use a combination of French and a made-up charades language to convey that copying the muse's look would require cutting all of the princess's hair off. She giggled again and nodded to indicate agreement.

I combed her beautiful hair all back into a ponytail that I held in one hand. With the other, I picked up my scissors, took a deep breath, and cut it off. I wondered what form of capital punishment would be used to execute me. I handed the cut ponytail to the servant and she carefully laid it on the vanity as though it was alive. The princess giggled. The servant was several shades paler. Hey, this wasn't exactly heart surgery!

When I finished cutting the princess's hair, the servant jumped into action, cleaning off the princess with a soft brush. Other young girls rushed in to sweep up and tidy everything.

Then came the makeup—light skin tone, powdered, matte, dark purple eyes with some sparkle glitz in the center of the eye, and dark but very matte lips. When I finished, the princess picked up the drawing, and held it next to her face. She smiled and nodded. She liked it. Maybe I wouldn't be executed after all!

The princess spoke to the servant, got up, and left the room.

"The princess would like you to wait and look at her clothes," the servant informed me. "She wants you to tell her what is not in fashion in Paris anymore."

I was going to get a look at the princess's wardrobe. This was going to be such fun. The princess returned to the room and I was shocked. She was wearing a black burka all the way to the floor. Her head was covered and she wore a solid gold mask that had been formed to fit the contours of her face.

She walked to a wall of collapsible closet doors and opened them. Inside, the closet was packed with dresses, gowns, and other outfits from every famous designer in the world.

One by one, she removed the outfits and held them up against her body. I would look at it for a moment and shake my head, yes or no. A "yes" would prompt her to return the garment to the closet. A "no" meant it would be tossed into a pile on the floor. I loved this game. I could play it all day.

After we went through each outfit, the servant clapped her hands. Young girls appeared and removed the pile of clothes from the floor. I couldn't imagine what they would do with them. I doubted that they called the Salvation Army for a pickup!

The princess then moved to another wall of closets and opened the doors to reveal shoes, lots of shoes. Each pair was shown to me for approval or rejection.

Then came the jewels. Cases from every top jeweler were opened for my inspection—diamond necklaces and earrings, emeralds, rubies. I was astonished. I wasn't about to say no to any of them. Then again, maybe I should have, and returned later dressed as the garbage collector!

When we were all finished, the princess thanked me, addressing me through her servant, and left the room. I realized that I had been looking directly at her the whole time, but at that point, who cared. I felt like her buddy now. The servant woman then reached into the sleeves of her kimono-like robe and from some secret pocket pulled out a small box.

In French, she told me that the princess was very pleased and wanted me to accept this gift for my wife. I had no wife, but took the gift anyway, and asked her to thank the princess. Next, she pulled out another small box and said that the princess wanted me to accept this gift for my mistress. I had no mistress either, but accepted the box. Then, she pulled out a third small box and said that the princess wanted me to accept this gift for myself. I asked her to thank the princess and took the box. After all that, she went to a drawer in the vanity and pulled out an envelope. This was my fee. I accepted it as well.

The servant then packed my hair and makeup supplies and I was back in the Rolls on my way to the airport. My bags from the apartment were already in the car. I received my passport and was back on the private jet headed for Paris. That's when I finally opened the gifts.

For my "mistress" there was a fine gold chain with a small gold birdcage. Inside the birdcage was a pearl. My "wife" received the same gift, but in place of the pearl was a small diamond. I couldn't help thinking that this was a direct reflection of how the princess must have viewed her life. A beautiful pearl or a diamond trapped inside a golden cage. My gift was a pair of gold cufflinks. The envelope contained $16,000.00 in American, hundred dollar bills.

Life in Paris was fun. I was working every day, and I felt that I was on top of the world. I partied a lot, but always had a good work ethic, arriving for all my appointments on time.

I always worked on editorial photo shoots and traveled to places like Munich and Zurich to earn the money I needed to live.

Editorial work never paid much, but there was a system in place where, once you were working with the top magazines, you could sell your credits. This meant that my agent could call the large makeup companies and tell them that the credit on the cover of whatever fashion magazine could read Danny Velasco for Whatever Makeup Company. The makeup companies would place a bid with my agent and the highest bidder would get the credit. It didn't really matter what products were used on the model's face, nor was it ever questioned.

The makeup company who won the bid would contact the magazine to inform them that they had bought the credit. Rough copies of the photos that would be used in the magazine were then sent to the company by messenger.

The makeup company could then match the colors of the eye shadows, blushers, lip gloss, and foundation to color names in its own line of cosmetics. Once that was done, they would contact the magazine with color names and the credit would read something like this, "Danny Velasco for Whatever Makeup Company. Danny Velasco used Soft Opal on the lips and Pink Glow on the cheeks, etc."

It was all fake, but that's how I made money.

Having my name in the magazine credits would also prompt advertisers to pay top dollar for my services. The more often my name appeared in the top magazines, the more work I would get with top advertisers for big money.

My rate continued to climb with each new job.

During one month, 13 of the covers on the Paris newsstands were my work. I had a friend photograph me holding them all fanned out in both hands.

To make immediate cash, I would try to work at least two weeks a month in Germany because Germans paid cash at the end of every job. Since my work regularly appeared in German *Vogue*, the German, Austrian, and Swiss advertisers were more than happy to have me available to do hair and makeup on their ads.

German *Vogue* also had an advertising department that created ads for many of the clients who advertised in the magazine. *Vogue* would book hair, makeup, models, and photographers. I was a regular and therefore got chosen very often for these gigs.

I would fly into Munich early in the morning, work for a week or two, and then fly home. If I wanted to be back in Paris for some party or dinner, I could fly home in the early evening and fly back to Munich in the morning. The flight was only a little over an hour. However, flying into Munich was one of the most frightening experiences one could ever have because the airport is at the base of the Alps. This means that the plane flies over hundreds of miles of desolate, deserted, snow-covered mountains, and suddenly it takes a nosedive and swoops down to come in for a landing. The plane rocks and shudders because of the turbulent winds whipping around the mountains. Many times, while the plane was landing, I felt as if my heart would jump out of my chest.

For that reason, I hated going to Munich in the winter, but the mountains were covered with snow all year round. If the plane were to crash, it would be highly unlikely that any passengers would survive. And even if they did survive, they wouldn't last more than a few hours before freezing to death.

My fears of crashing in the Alps were alleviated when someone told me about the midnight train to Munich. It left Paris every night at midnight and arrived in Munich at 7AM. I began to book my trips using the train. I reserved a private sleeper car, so I could sleep all the way. A porter would take my passport for the customs when I got on the train and show it to border police without waking me up. I could take off my clothes, hang them up, and not worry about anything. Each private sleeper car had a sink with running water and underneath that sink was a small flushable toilet that would swing out and swing back under the sink. It was perfect.

The porter would wake passengers up one hour before arrival with hot coffee, a croissant, and the stamped passport on the tray. There was enough time to get myself ready, and by the time the train pulled into the Munich railway station, I was rested and ready to start the day.

I loved to go clubbing in Munich at P1 Nightclub. It was a disco located underneath the Haus der Kunst Museum. It had a private entrance around the side, and the building sat on many acres of land along the Isar River.

This river is a trip. It runs right through the heart of the city. In the summer, business people came to eat lunch along its banks. They took off all their clothes and carefully placed them out on the grass. Then they ate their lunch and lay in the sun. It was like a nudist colony. The Germans are very comfortable with nudity. Even the saunas at all the gyms are co-ed.

P1 always had the most beautiful people in the world. It was almost as good as Studio 54. I would always meet up with people I knew there. So, whatever plans I had earlier in the evening, be it dinner with friends or just back to my small hotel for a nap after work, I would always end up at P1 at the end of the night.

I worked for some young fashion designers in Munich, and one night they took me to a punk rock bar. Punk was strong in Germany. The Germans seemed to love the dark clothes with lots of buckles and straps.

Black lipstick and black eyes on "dead white" faces seemed to be the rage, even for the men. The hair was straight and dyed black, with accents of bright blue, red, yellow, and orange. They used silk dyes to get the primary colors, and soap mixed with gel to get the hair to stand out in irregular angles from their heads.

It was a visual extravaganza and I was like a sponge, taking it all in. I got lots of ideas for hair and makeup (if you can believe that!). I toned down and tamed these looks quite a bit, and used them in my work. The result was beautiful but super edgy. Young German designers loved it.

Back in Paris, anything that was new and different in fashion seemed to work. I had one friend who really made me laugh. She used to mix colors herself to come up with blends that she couldn't get in makeup stores. She told me that, one day, she just got this idea and mixed a larger than normal batch of yellow color, took the entire bowl, and poured it over the model's head.

Everyone looked horrified for a few seconds as the paint dripped down the model's face and neck, and spilled on her outfit. Everyone then looked at the designer with baited breath to see his reaction. When the designer said, "Fabulous, I love it," everyone's shoulders must have relaxed.

So, my friend mixed up other colors and poured them over all the models' heads. I laughed until I cried when I heard about it. Two months later, these photos were published and she became the most popular makeup artist of the hour. She became known as "BOLD" and "DARING!"

Later, she told me that she could have poured pork and beans over their heads, and they would have loved it.

I still think it's the funniest thing I have ever heard in this business.

Another time, she was making up a model who was giving her a hard time. My friend got so upset that she took her black eyeliner pencil and wrote across the model's forehead a five-letter word usually used to describe a female dog. The designer thought this was awesome and made the model leave it on her forehead when she was photographed. Then the makeup artist wrote on every model's face one word that she felt described her. Two months later these photos were published, and again she was hailed as "BOLD" and "DARING!"

Again, I thought this was hilarious. Like I said, in Paris, anything that was new and different seemed to work.

Yes, I was living on top of the world—in with the "In Crowd," as they say. There was always the "club of the moment" in Paris, but I preferred to go to house parties.

One night, I was at one of those house parties. At some point, a guy came up to me and asked if I wanted to do a "line." I knew this meant a line of cocaine, because I had been using cocaine for a long time.

"Go to the bedroom," he said.

I did. A group of people were gathered around a mirror lying on a dresser. One by one, they took the rolled up $100 dollar bill that was handed to them, bent over the mirror, and sniffed a line off it. I took my turn.

As I bent over the mirror, I noticed that the lines were of a brown powder. This was curious because any cocaine I had ever seen was white. I sniffed it anyway.

"I have never seen brown cocaine," I said to the guy who had invited me into the bedroom.

"That wasn't cocaine. It was heroin," he replied, in his heavy French accent.

Heroin! *Oh well,* I thought, *at least it's something new*!

Within a few minutes, a feeling of total calm came over my body. It was a warm, relaxed feeling and I loved it. So, this was the "big bad" heroin? This wasn't such a big deal. This was how I had always wanted to feel. I floated through the rest of the evening in a dreamy surreal fog. The following day, I managed to locate the dealer and I was at his apartment buying more of the drug. This was my initiation to heroin and for the next 15 years, I would never be without it.

I saw the dealer as often as possible. I would buy large amounts of the drug so that it would last for a long time. Often, I bought drugs when I still had a large supply at home, because I was scared to be without it. I began to plan my days around meetings with the dealer.

You could say that I was hooked from my very first taste of heroin. I would go to work high every day, and my work never seemed to be affected. In fact, I thought I did my job even better on heroin. I was more relaxed and more willing to try new things.

Maybe that was just an illusion, but I believed it to be true. It somehow seemed to justify my addiction. In reality, the heroin just helped mask the deep loneliness and void in my heart. I was numb to feelings that I didn't want to feel. As a matter of fact, I felt nothing at all.

CHAPTER 7

America: Back Home

*A man can do nothing better than to eat and
drink and find satisfaction in his work.*
ECCLESIASTES 2: 24

F ive years seemed to go by very quickly. I had traveled all over
the world, and now I was homesick. Paris was good to me. My
career skyrocketed there and was now solid. I had what seemed on
the outside to be a great life, but there was a deep void inside me. I
longed to wake up and speak English.

There were so many things I missed—the cabbies screaming out the
windows of the cabs, the sounds of the New York streets. A friend from
school who once visited the Big Apple described it best; she said she loved
hearing music in the streets and people speaking in all the languages. Paris
was a great city, but it wasn't as cosmopolitan as New York.

I missed the view of Manhattan from either the Queens side of
the river or the Kosciuszko Bridge leading into Brooklyn. And few
sights are as thrilling as the Manhattan skyline. During the day, the
skyscrapers are truly majestic, rising up from the water like some
enormous stone creatures, firm, tall, and strong. New York sparkles
at night with millions of lights inviting you to come and explore,
offering you anything your heart desires.

It's alive both night and day.

I missed peanut butter.

I missed my family.

I missed everything American.

I just wanted to come home.

There was an emptiness that still ached in the middle of my soul.
I had the life I had always dreamed of, and I couldn't understand

why I was so unhappy and lonely. I had friends all over the world, but I was still suffering from deep loneliness. Even in the midst of everything and everybody, I always felt all alone.

No amount of friends, money, sex, travel, fame, drugs, or alcohol could fill that aching place deep inside of me. I couldn't figure out why people all around me seemed so happy all the time, while I was so miserable. I decided that maybe going back home was the answer. Wherever I happened to be, it seemed as if happiness was always someplace else.

I flew into JFK on a work trip. This job, even though it was being shot in New York, was for a French designer. The photo shoot was a series of ads for a new brand of cigarettes that had this designer's name on it. They are still around today, but this was the launch of the brand. I decided to take this opportunity to find the best New York agent and an apartment in which to live.

After going through customs at JFK Airport, I jumped into a taxi and headed to my brother's apartment. When I arrived, he said that I had a message on his answering machine. The voicemail was from Toni.

"Hey," she said perkily. "Welcome home. I can't wait to see you. Call me as soon as you get in. We need to talk about your future and how we can begin to book you on jobs here at home. Call me. Bye!"

I went cold. How did she know that I was coming home that day? It spooked me just to wonder how she had found out. Who did she have spying on me, keeping her informed? After all, I had been away for five years!

I knew that I had to see her and explain to her, once and for all, that our relationship was over. I would never again come back under her control or even work with her, for that matter—not under any circumstances. I decided that I had to talk to her immediately, just to have it behind me.

I walked out of my brother's apartment and took a cab directly to Toni's place. As I arrived to the block on which she lived, I found that the police had cordoned it off. Something bad had clearly happened to someone, and there was a lot of police activity. I got out of the cab as close to Toni's building as I could and walked through.

"What happened?" I asked someone on the street.

"Someone jumped! Suicide, I guess," the stranger answered. "They jumped from that floor up there."

I looked up. He was pointing at Toni's apartment window. It was opened and I could see police officers inside. I was informed by the stranger that the body had already been taken away. I didn't see any body, just the place where it had landed.

Was it Toni who had hit the sidewalk? I wondered. *Or did someone else jump from her window? Was it possible that someone pushed her, maybe somebody with whom she had drug dealings?* All these questions raced through my mind, as my heartbeat accelerated.

"It was a woman," someone else said.

Toni had called, asking me to phone or come by as soon as possible. Was this some kind of a sick joke? Did she plan this? Did she know that I would come right away and see this? Was it a coincidence, or what?

I will never know for sure, at least not in this life.

I returned to my brother's apartment in shock and disbelief, with a million questions running through my head.

Later that night, I connected with some of Toni's friends, who told me that she was broke and there wasn't even money to give her a decent burial.

How could she be so broke? I wondered, remembering her lavish lifestyle and all the money she used to throw around. None of her friends could understand or offer an answer. We all chipped in and paid for her funeral.

Toni was Jewish and Judaism regards suicide as a criminal act, akin to murder. Her death had been deemed a suicide, so she couldn't be buried near her parents. She was to be placed in a different part of the cemetery, a sort of Potter's Field, where she would be cast out for all eternity, because her religion couldn't tolerate suicide. It made me so very sad. True, I didn't want to work with her or even spend any time at all with her again, but I certainly didn't want any harm to come to her.

As shaken up as I was, I decided to put this tragic event behind me and go on with my life. I had an ability to put these kinds of things out of my mind and not deal with the feelings. I'd had a lot of practice at that as a child.

The old thoughts were resurfacing in my mind—women were as weak as flowers. Look, but don't pick them, because they will die. Again, this was proving to be true.

The agent that I met while on this trip to New York was a high-powered woman who represented a couple of top photographers, hairdressers, and makeup artists who were doing all the big accounts, as well as the best editorial jobs New York had to offer.

She flipped through my portfolio and asked, "How soon can I start booking you?"

"I have to return to Paris to fulfill several outstanding obligations," I said. "But I won't take any other jobs there. I'll call you with the dates."

We agreed to proceed that way. She set my day rate at $3,000.

Next, I set out to find a place to live. I was always willing to pay a little more than the average person, so I had the choice of many beautiful apartments. I finally decided on a 5,000-square-foot loft on Hudson Street in the Tribeca section of Manhattan. It was a state-of-the-art loft with two bedrooms, two baths, floor-to-ceiling windows—everything ultra-modern.

From my bed, I could look out on the World Trade Center buildings (at that time, they were still standing). Also, from my bed, I could—by just pushing a few buttons—fill my tub, adjust the water temperature, and start the Jacuzzi. The rent was several thousand a month, but I signed the lease without hesitation. I decided to buy the furniture later.

I returned to Paris, fulfilled my professional obligations, and flew back to New York. I decided to leave all my clothes and furniture in Paris. I wanted to keep the Paris apartment, so I would always have a place to stay when I had to return for work there.

I wanted to furnish my new loft in New York with mid-century modern furniture, and I only wanted the real deal, not imitations or reproductions.

Mid-Century Modern was a short period from about 1951 to 1959. It was called Furniture for Future Living. Space exploration was just starting back then, and furniture designers were preparing for the "space age." They were ahead of their time. Curiously enough, that style didn't sell well in the 50s, but now, 30 years later, it was highly collectable.

I contacted antique dealers of mid-century furniture and put several scouts on the lookout for original pieces at the auction houses they frequented. Within a few months, my apartment looked exactly the way I wanted it to look.

My living room was like a modern art sculpture garden. The sofa was a large pair of red lips designed by Salvatore Dali and modeled after Mae West's lips. (Later, this sofa was reissued as Marilyn Monroe's lips. I guess Mae West was a relic from the too distant past, and the manufactures who had bought the design figured it would sell better with a more current sex symbol.) It was bright red. You sat on the lower lip and leaned back on the upper lip. The originals were rare and very collectable.

The chairs scattered around the large open space of the living room were all classics. The Swan Chair and the Egg Chair were both designed by the famed Danish designer, Arne Jacobsen. There were also two Ribbon Chairs and Ribbon Footstools by the French designer, Pierre Paulin. All the chests of drawers were designed and manufactured by the German furniture designer, Vladimir Kagan.

In the kitchen, all of my plates, serving platters, bowls, cups, and saucers were designed by the American industrial designer, Russell Wright. I also had settings for 12 in every color in which he ever made them. My silverware was original Georg Jensen (a Danish silversmith) from the same period.

Today, this furniture is almost untouchable. Even if you can find the original pieces, they would cost a fortune. I didn't need a lot of furniture because the loft was so architecturally beautiful.

I began to paint canvases in oil again, as I had done when I was younger, so most of the paintings on the wall were mine. I hung one of my works of a left eye on the wall right behind the lips sofa, but I hung it near the ceiling in the approximate location where an eye would be in relation to the lips. I also painted very stylized portraits of my closest friends. I could paint all alone for hours on end.

I was all set and loved my new digs. I was home again. That's all that mattered right now. My new agent had no problem getting me work. I never skipped a beat.

I also didn't skip a beat finding new drug dealers in New York. I quickly found the best drugs the city had to offer. The Lower East Side was a drug supermarket. I would put on my jeans and an old jacket and hit the streets. Buying drugs was as easy as buying a pack of cigarettes.

I wasn't the type of person who took an aggressive approach to getting work. Well, maybe that's not quite true. It was my agent's job to be aggressive, but I was aggressively pushing her for the best jobs. My agent would contact prospective clients, my portfolio would go out to them by messenger, and I would usually get the job for which they were hiring.

I would be asked by my agent which photographers I wanted to meet, and she would contact their studios and arrange for my portfolio to be sent to them. If they liked my work and had jobs coming up, a deal would be struck, and I would get the details of the jobs. Then I would purchase whatever was needed for that job—if anything—and I would show up the day of the job, ready to work.

There was one photographer in particular that I wanted to work with. I loved her style and I thought the sense of beauty and fantasy in her photos was the best in the business. I told my agent that—no matter what—I wanted to meet her and work with her. My agent phoned the studio and was told that no portfolios were being seen at that time. This photographer had all the hair and makeup talent she wanted and was not considering anyone new. I was beside myself.

She wouldn't even look at my work! How dare she! I jumped into a taxi and went to my agent's office.

"Give me my portfolio and the address of this studio," I said.

I took my portfolio, the photographer's address, and jumped into another taxi. I arrived at the address, went up the elevator, and walked right into her studio. The receptionist asked if she could help me.

I told her my name was Danny Velasco; I wanted to see her boss and show her my portfolio.

"I spoke to your agent earlier today and told her that we aren't seeing any portfolios at this time," she informed me. "Besides, she is not even here."

I pulled out my portfolio, handed it over the desk, and said to her, "You look through this portfolio, and when you are finished, if you think I am not right for your boss, I will leave. But if you think my work is right for her, take it and show it to her now. I happen to know that she is here."

I was bluffing. I had no idea if she was there or not.

The receptionist took my portfolio and opened it. She flipped through it quickly and what seemed to be half-heartedly. I was getting a little nervous. Maybe I would be shot down. Suddenly, she closed the portfolio and got up. She put the portfolio under her arm and told me to take a seat. She disappeared into another part of the studio.

A few minutes later, the photographer herself walked out with my portfolio in one hand, with the other hand extended to me.

I shook her hand and she said, "Your portfolio is beautiful. I have some jobs coming up that you would be perfect for. We will call your agent and book it. Thanks for coming by."

"Thank you for looking at it," I answered.

She turned to walk away and then turned back. "How did you know I was here?" she asked.

"I didn't," I answered.

She smiled and disappeared into the studio.

Once outside, I called my agent to tell her that I had gotten the photographer to look at my book.

"I know," my agent answered. "They've already called and booked you on three campaigns."

"There will be more to come," I said.

My first booking with this new photographer was that weekend. I was to show up at 9PM in front of the courthouse in downtown Manhattan. *Strange time and place for a photo shoot,* I thought.

I arrived at what appeared to be more of a movie set than a photo shoot. There were trailers with equipment and dozens of people moving around. Security was everywhere.

"Are you hair and makeup?" someone asked.

"Yes," I answered.

"Go right into the rotunda of the courthouse. That's where hair, makeup, and wardrobe are."

I wondered what the cost was to "hire" the municipal courthouse as a set.

Inside was a flurry of activity. People were running around carrying huge ball gowns. Racks of clothing rolled by and mostly white people everywhere.

Other hairdressers and makeup artists were already working on the many people who would be in this photo shoot. Beautiful women, children, and men sat around, waiting for their turns. Other people were trying on clothes behind screens that were set up as makeshift dressing rooms.

The photographer spotted me and came over to say hello.

"Set up where you can and we will bring better lighting and a mirror for you to work with." She talked fast. "I want you to work on the main model. We will show you her gown when we decide what she will be wearing, and after that, you can begin hair and makeup. It will be a long while before we actually shoot this thing. After I have chosen the entire wardrobe for all the models, I'm going outside to start lighting the steps and front of the building. Everything will be shot on the steps of the courthouse. We can shoot until the sun comes up and after that we can't shoot anymore. Have fun and be creative!"

She turned and walked away. She seemed to be in complete control of all the chaos. I was excited. *This is one for the book*, I thought. And, now, I guess I was right! It *is* in the book.

Hours went by. The model I was responsible for looked like a dream. I had done her makeup in a colorful fantasy. Yellow, orange, and burnt red colors on her face—something I had never done before. I wanted this photographer to be impressed with my work.

I styled the model's hair very big and extreme, larger than life. The wardrobe stylist dressed her in what looked like a ball gown that was meant to be worn in some king's court in some distant past. The gown was all white, with giant balloon sleeves that ended at the cuffs with lace and lots of buttons. It had a large white taffeta skirt with layers upon layers of crinoline underneath it. It was covered with pearls and white sequins that glittered in the lights.

She was magnificent. Beautiful children dressed in high court dresses from some long-ago era held the reins of a white stallion, while another child played with a white python. Everyone was dressed in all white.

Outside, the steps had been lit in primary colors of yellow and blue. Smoke machines diffused the light and made everything look unearthly. It was a surreal vision and attention had been paid to every detail. Small mirrors had even been set up on stands to reflect beams of light directly into the models' faces, so that their eyes glowed in some kind of supernatural way.

I was not just excited to be part of this shoot, but also mesmerized and impressed by what had been created here. This photographer's vision was like no other in the business. She was by far the most brilliant artist I had ever met.

This is how I had always wanted to work—a large, over-the-top, super fantasy, while creating with no boundaries. I went home in the morning wondering what could possibly top this.

Many more great jobs did come my way. Along with big jobs came big money. Big money allowed me not only to have a great life, but also enabled my drug use to spiral out of control.

PART TWO

My Detour Through Hell

CHAPTER 8

The Dual Life

When I surveyed all that my hands had done and what I
had toiled to achieve, everything was meaningless, a chasing
after the wind, nothing was gained under the sun.
ECCLESIASTES 2:11

L ife seemed to be going in two directions at the same time. My career skyrocketed and my personal life plummeted.

During the day, I was working with the most beautiful faces in the world and with superstar celebrities. At night, I was walking the streets of New York's Lower East Side looking for drugs.

When I had to travel on world tours with some high profile rock star, I carried enough drugs to get a small nation high. I never had to worry about crossing borders with drugs. Our private plane would usually land on some back runway and cars would drive out to meet us. Custom officials would come on board and stamp all the passports, get an autograph from the celebrity, accept a token of appreciation, and that was it. Limousines would drive us out of the airport through a back gate.

Sometimes, we drove by the hotel where we would be staying, and if fans and paparazzi waited outside, we would continue driving to another location. From there, we were taken via underground tunnels into the hotel's basement. We would be met by security and hotel management and escorted up to the suites via private back elevators.

Bodyguards would always surround us whenever we moved from one location to another. It was as if we were traveling in a small bubble of our own, totally isolated from the rest of the world. Being in a celebrity's entourage was nothing to complain about. I never had to deal with the real world and I could just drift through life, going wherever I was led.

I never figured out how fans and paparazzi knew where a celebrity would be going next. But it seemed that they were always one step ahead of us. My life on these tours was controlled by the group I was with, and, of course, by drugs.

I had everything that I had always dreamed of. On the outside, it was a perfect career. Anyone getting into this business would say, "That's the kind of career I want."

Meanwhile, I was more and more miserable. I just couldn't shake off the unhappiness, loneliness, and emptiness that had permeated my heart and soul. But I seemed to have the antidote, at least a temporary one—heroin. It allowed me not to feel anything. I was emotionally dead. Life had no meaning for me anyway.

I knew that one day my life would be over, and that was fine with me. I was so depressed and numb, I really didn't care if I lived or died, but I didn't have the guts to kill myself.

I would travel from country to country, sometimes not even knowing what country I was in, or what day of the week it was. Nothing mattered to me.

On the road, our lives were planned and regulated down to the tiniest detail. We were told what time to get up; what time to be ready; what time to have our bags by the door of our hotel rooms; what time the cars would arrive to pick us up; what time they needed the celebrity ready; when we would eat; where we would eat; and with whom we would eat. If we needed anything, all we had to do was ask, and we would always get it. We could mindlessly go from day to day for weeks on end. We were only expected to do our assigned jobs and follow orders. If you could do that, you were valuable to the team, and everyone was happy.

One night, back in New York, just as I was going to pay a dealer on the street for 10 bags of heroin, we were suddenly surrounded by undercover police officers with their guns drawn. I was thrown against the wall of a building, legs spread, my hands pulled behind my back, and cuffed. I couldn't believe it.

I was put into a police van and taken to Central Booking. I was fingerprinted and photographed. I was put into a holding cell with everyone else who was arrested that night—about 100 guys, all cuffed, charged with every kind of crime imaginable, waiting to see a judge. I waited about 72 hours.

In the holding cell, I got violently sick. I had a fever. I felt like I had a bad flu and was hit by a truck. I was in full withdrawal from heroin. Every orifice of my body was trying to push out the drug. *So this is what it feels like to be without the drug,* I thought. I had never gone into full withdrawal before. That sweet warm feeling that the drug gave me now morphed into a monster that was very angry for not being fed. Withdrawal racked my body. The pain in my legs was unbearable. The vomiting was uncontrollable. My body shook and jerked violently.

I covered my head with my coat, and lay on the floor of the holding cell. The cool floor, even though it was filthy, felt good against my hot, feverish forehead.

When I finally stood before the judge, he lectured me about drug abuse and then let me go. I didn't know it at the time, but this was the first of several arrests.

Unfortunately, the arrest, jail time, and horrific withdrawal symptoms did not leave any lasting impression on me. On my way home from court, I stopped in the same area where I had been previously arrested and bought more drugs.

Back at work, it was as if the last several days in a jail cell never happened. The jobs I was getting were great. One good job led to another.

Everyone on a film crew usually works on a freelance basis. As art directors, photographers, wardrobe stylists, etc., move from one job to another, they might talk about your work and recommend you to the next job. Eventually, it all snowballs on you.

I landed a deal with an advertising company that handled all the work for a very big American cosmetics company, as well as several other large accounts. It wasn't an actual signed contract, but more of a verbal agreement. They had guaranteed me "X" number of work days at $3,000 per day, with the understanding that they had first option on my time. I was to check with them before taking any other bookings.

This verbal agreement did not, however, limit who I could work for under the unspoken "conflict of interest" rule. I had been recommended by the photographer who was shooting a cosmetics job, and also by the model who was under contract to this particular company. This model also had "the last say" on who did her make-up for any ad in which she appeared.

She had spoken highly of me when she heard that I was being considered for the job. As a result of her recommendation, I was hired. These were some of the most beautiful ads and TV commercials I had ever worked on to date. One of the TV commercials even won the Clio Award that year. The Clio Award is sort of the Academy Award for TV commercials.

This led to even bigger and better jobs. I began to work with very high profile rock stars and a country and western diva who loved lots of makeup. This country and western singer was, and still is, the greatest singer and humanitarian to ever come out of Tennessee. Without mentioning any names, I want to tell about my first meeting with her.

I was asked by Revlon to fly to Tennessee and do her makeup for the launch of her new cosmetics line that Revlon had formulated for her and was promoting with her. I arrived at her family home, a walled-off estate encompassing almost an entire mountain in the Smokies.

I was told that she had her own hairdresser who worked only for her, and he flew from one of her houses to another, just washing and styling her many wigs that were housed in each home.

I got to the estate and was surprised to find a two-room shack, which I was later told had been reproduced from photographs of the original abode where she had grown up. The difference was that the inside of this shack had been modernized considerably.

The new shack had running water; the original didn't.

The new one had central air and heat. The old one didn't.

The new one had a bathroom. The old one didn't.

The new one had a floor. The old one didn't.

The new one had a kitchen. The old one had just a fireplace.

I was very impressed with this person who had held on to her old values and set things up to give her the comforts of those memories, albeit modernized with the new amenities.

After setting up my makeup equipment, I went outside to wait for her to arrive. Finally, a black Ford Bronco came through the gates and pulled up to the house. The driver came around to the passenger side and opened the door.

Suddenly, this tiny version of the celebrity I thought of as bigger than life stepped out of the car. When I say tiny, I mean she was very petite. At least, *most* of her was very petite. Some parts, however, were very, very large. The first thing I thought of was that she would never fall flat on her face, if you know what I mean.

She walked across the lawn and up the steps of the porch. She smiled beautifully, held out her hand, and said, "You must be Danny!"

I thought that she was the most beautiful woman I had ever seen. It was as if her beauty was something more than just her outer appearance. It seemed to shine and radiate through her. She was dazzling.

We walked into the house and into the bedroom where we would be doing her makeup. Mind you, she was already completely made up. She said to me that before I removed her makeup and reapplied it for the filming she wanted to tell me a story. This is what she told me:

"Danny, when I was a little girl, I grew up right here on this mountain and in this house. Once a week, daddy would go to town to buy food and supplies. All my brothers, sisters, and I loved going to town with daddy, but there were so many of us that we had to take turns. I loved when it was my turn to go. I always looked for a lady I often saw there who I thought was the most beautiful lady I had even seen. I used to think, 'When I grow up, I want to look just like her.' Well, one day, I went to town with my daddy and I didn't see that lady any more. When I mentioned to my daddy that I didn't see her in town that day, he said that it was because she was the town tramp, and she had been run out of town. And, Danny, even though I never saw her again, I still want to look just like her."

I smiled. She was the most charming woman I had ever met. I painted her face based on my idea of what the town tramp looked like, but throwing in a little class. She loved it, and we got along just great.

While I was making her up, my stomach began to growl from hunger. I was so excited to meet her that I had forgotten to eat breakfast. The following morning, when I arrived to start her makeup again, she said, "Before we start, I've fixed you breakfast. Now sit down and eat." I couldn't believe that she, the big celebrity, actually had made me breakfast. I told her as much.

"Wait till my friends hear that you fixed me breakfast," I said, excitedly. "They won't believe it!"

She stood leaning against the kitchen sink, eating pork bellies out of a can. "Well," she retorted. "I don't want to hear that grumbly ole stomach of yours in my ear again today!"

I remember thinking to myself, *Here is the most famous country western star in the world, barefoot, wearing a white terry bathrobe, a white terry towel on her head, five-inch-high heel slippers with big foo foo pompoms on the top, leaning against a sink eating canned pork bellies after fixing me a big breakfast. Unbelievable!*

I ended up working with her quite a few times after that. I looked forward to seeing her, and enjoyed each time I was with her. I could tell you a dozen stories about her, because I was always so impressed by this lady. And she never changed her personality or demeanor. Some celebrities project one image when meeting them and another one under different circumstances. But she was always the same—consistently nice. This was what I loved most about her—she was always the same person no matter what the situation was, what time of the day or night it was, or who she was with.

Another client of mine was a lady who had been married to a very famous director and now was the editor-in-chief of her own magazine. Whenever I was in New York City, she would have her limousine pick me up every morning at 5:30 AM and drive me to her Park Avenue apartment. I would arrive at 6AM, and coffee would be waiting for me. She would come out of her bathroom in a robe, with a white towel wrapped on her head, and sit in front of a mirror in her dressing area.

I would towel off her hair and blow it dry. Then I would apply very light, very natural makeup on her. She would thank me and disappear into her bedroom, while I packed up and left.

Her driver would then take me back home, or to my photo shoot if I had an early studio call. I did that every day, Monday through Friday. She paid me $750 a week for this service, which meant regardless of whether I worked at any other job that week, I would still receive a check and always be home by 7AM. She later died of cancer and that ended this gig.

Life is funny. When one door closes, another one usually opens. I had lots of doors open for me.

There was the time when a rock star, who is still around today, hired me to work on his rock videos. He was known for his very sexual songs and was always connected romantically to many women in Hollywood. Once, he flew me to Los Angeles for 28 days to work on a series of videos that would be released, one at a time, as songs from his latest album were released.

He was a strange guy and rarely spoke to me, but he managed to get me to work not only with him, but also with all the singers who were friends of his. He seemed to be the best publicity person I had at the time.

Each day of shooting was very long and drawn out. Sixteen and 18-hour days were usual. He danced through most of the videos, and I wondered how he got the energy to keep going. Our schedule was three days of work, one day off. We would work late into the night and have what is called "short turnarounds," which meant we had to be back on set four hours after we were released for the day. Of course, they made it worth my while with phenomenal pay.

Each time I would arrive back at the hotel, I would have many messages from a woman I didn't even know. She sounded very nice, always said she knew how hard I must be working, but would love a return phone call from me.

On my second day off from our shooting schedule, I decided to return her many phone calls. She answered the phone and when she heard my name she said, "Oh, the famous Danny Velasco! I feel so honored that you called me back. Finally, I get to speak to the famous Danny Velasco!" Every red flag in me went up.

"I'm sorry, but I'm not sure I know you," I replied.

"Well, we have never met, but I sure know all about you," she said. "I'm a journalist for (she mentioned the name of a tabloid) and we want to do an exclusive interview with you. You're the makeup artist to the stars. I know about your work with (she mentioned some well-known celebrities) and know you went here with so and so, and were there with so and so." She had obviously done her homework and knew about everyone with whom I had ever worked, and everything I had ever done in my career.

"I can do an interview with you at your convenience, and I have been authorized by my newspaper to offer you $50,000 in cash," she said. "As a matter of fact, I can come and meet you right now."

"Oh, I get it! You don't really want to interview *me*. You just want me to give you dirt on the celebrities I work with," I said.

"No, we want to do an exclusive interview with *you*," she quickly answered. "If you want to talk about the celebrities you work with, that is up to you. But, of course, the whole point of the interview is because you do work with famous celebrities. So, anything you have to say about them would be good for the interview."

"Lady," I retorted, "if I did an interview with you, I would probably never work in this business again. I would be giving up my career for $50,000. Does that sound reasonable to you?"

"Well, I'm sure I can get you more money after the interview—all in cash. Do we have a deal?"

"No, we don't have a deal. Don't ever call me again," I said and hung up.

One of the most valuable assets in my business is discretion. I was privy to so much "insider" information on these celebrities. If I didn't keep my mouth shut, I could kiss my career goodbye.

One morning, I arrived at a photo studio, and the model with whom I was working that day was a very beautiful redhead who was with Ford Models in New York. She was sweet and we hit it off immediately. She told me she was also a singer.

"Really?" I asked. "I work with a lot of singers."

That's when she told me she "sang for the Lord."

Sang for the Lord? What did that mean? She told me that she sang in her very large church choir, which had even won several Grammy Awards.

"They give Grammy Awards for 'singing for the Lord?'" I asked incredulously. I almost started laughing.

Ever since my mother's death, I had remained very skeptical of religion. It was not exactly an integral part of my life. She was, however, very sincere and continued talking about the Lord. I remember thinking, "Man, this girl is beautiful, but she's a religious fanatic!"

"Hey, I don't know anything about the Lord!" I said flippantly.

Wanda Geddie was her name and before she left that day, she said to me, "Hey, Danny, I know who you are—a famous hairdresser and makeup artist. I know your work in all the big magazines and with famous celebrities. But you're in trouble."

"Yeah, who isn't in trouble?" I said.

"Can I pray for you?" was her answer to this question.

"Sure, you can pray for me, anytime you want," I said, still not taking her seriously.

I thought she would go home and before going to bed maybe would bow her head, say a little prayer, make the sign of the cross, and that would be it. But, that was not what she did.

Right there, she took my hands into hers and began to pray out loud. I was dumbfounded and embarrassed. I looked around to see who was watching.

Oh my goodness! This woman is a nut, I thought.

After she prayed, she looked at me and said, "Danny, the day you call on the name of the Lord, He's going to set you free."

I looked at her in amazement. "Really, the problem is that I will never 'CALL ON THE NAME OF THE LORD!'" I said mockingly. I really believed that to be true.

Wanda smiled and invited me to come by her church sometime and hear the choir sing. I declined that offer. *I will never go to a church again as long as I live,* I thought. *I'd had enough of that as a child, and what good did it do?*

About a week later, I walked into a studio and there she was again — still smiling; still talking about the Lord; still wanting to pray for me; still reminding me to call on the name of the Lord; and still inviting me to visit her church.

I remained adamant. There was no way I was going to visit her church. I decided long ago that church was not for me. I believed in God, I think, but all the rules and restrictions that went with organized religion had no place in my life. It was a crutch for weak people. And who wanted to hear a choir sing anyway? I hung out with real, famous singers, and even they didn't matter much to me.

So what if someone had a good voice? That didn't mean he or she was any better than anyone else. Everyone was good at something. If you could sing, you cashed in and made loads of money. You didn't "SING FOR THE LORD!" That only meant to me that you did it for free — a waste of time and talent.

Slowly, but surely, things started going downhill for me. Drugs were beginning to affect my work life. My actual work didn't seem to suffer at all. As a matter of fact, people said that it was better than ever. But the drugs did begin to have an impact on other areas of my professional life.

For example, once I was staying at the Biltmore Hotel in Coral Gables, Florida, for a couple of weeks while working there. The rooms at the Biltmore are famous for their opulent décor and top-notch service. The Biltmore is a very large, pink hotel in the style of an old-world luxury spa. At the time when the Biltmore opened, it boasted the largest pool, I believe, in the United States. It's said that Johnny Weissmuller spent all his free time swimming laps there. (He was famous for being a five-time Olympic Gold medalist in the 1920s, and also the movie Tarzan in the 1930s).

During my stay at the Biltmore, I was in bed and fell asleep (or maybe I should say that I nodded off while high on heroin), with a cigarette in my hand. I woke up to my bedspread in flames, right over my chest. There was a pitcher of water by my bed. I grabbed it, poured its entire contents on the bedspread, putting out the fire.

The next day, the hotel manager called me into his office. He yelled at me, saying that these bedspreads were very valuable, one of a kind, etc. I apologized to him, sarcastically reminding him that was the purpose of insurance.

As incredible as it sounds, the next night I woke up to my new bedspread on fire. Again, I poured water on it and managed to extinguish it. I guess I hadn't learned my lesson, because I then reached for another cigarette and must have nodded off with that one too. When I awoke in the morning, I looked down at the carpet next to the bed. I saw one of my cigarette filters in the middle of a large circular burn hole about a foot and a half wide where the carpet had smoldered.

I thought, *Oh, no! What in the world will I tell the hotel manager when this gets reported?*

I tried pushing the bed over the burn hole, but found that the headboard was nailed to the wall. The bed shifted over but the headboard didn't.

It may sound funny now as I write this, but I remember the despair I felt at that time. At about 10 o'clock, a young bell hop dressed in a dark purple uniform complete with a cap and epaulettes came running towards the group I was shooting with on the grounds of the Biltmore. He informed me that the hotel manager wanted to speak with me immediately.

When I entered the office, the manager began to yell at me at the top of his lungs. He threatened me with arrest. In the end, I had to have thousands of dollars wired to the hotel, in order to not have the manager call the police and have me charged with arson. It was a nightmare.

Around that time, I had met a girl named Mica who lived in Texas, but who came often to New York. She was the niece of a commercial film director with whom I frequently worked. She and I became really good friends. Mica loved her drugs and would develop a very violent temper when she drank alcohol. It was as if another, much angrier person took over. She would flip from one personality to another in an instant—from sweet and funny to a vicious, foul-mouthed monster. Her Jekyll-Hyde personality switch fascinated me.

One long weekend, she was staying with me at my loft and when I got home from working all day, I noticed that she had been drinking.

"Call your family in Florida. It's urgent," she said, in her angry "Ms. Hyde" voice. I knew that something was wrong—first, by her nasty attitude, and second, because my family almost never called with urgent messages. I got on the phone right away and called my dad's house. My stepsister answered the phone, crying.

"Dad is dead," she sobbed. "We were watching TV and he just stood up and then dropped dead. I tried to revive him, but I couldn't. I let him die. I let him die."

I was shocked. My father was dead? How was it possible that he had died so suddenly? We had remained very close, speaking on the phone often. I knew he had a bad heart and had suffered a few minor heart attacks already, but I couldn't believe that he had died at the age of 53.

I put my own disarray aside and tried to calm down my stepsister, but I couldn't comfort her.

"I'll be down on the first plane in the morning," I told her.

I could hear Mica mumbling and talking to herself still in her "Ms Hyde" persona.

"Sure, drop dead now. Why not spoil my weekend in New York?" she muttered. "Could have died any time, but why not now—might as well spoil my weekend. Who cares about me? I spent a lot of money to be here this weekend. Might as well do it now… so, what will I do now… who cares about what I'll do now."

I couldn't believe how insensitive she was! She actually raged on like this, completely oblivious to the tragedy that had just struck my family, or, for that matter, my own grief.

I turned around and yelled, "Shut up! My father just died. Could you think about someone other than yourself for a change?"

"Sure... who the hell cares that they screw up my weekend!" she screamed.

I got so angry that I grabbed her by the arm and literally walked her out of my apartment, into the elevator, and out on to the street. I then went back upstairs and tossed her clothes, suitcases, and toiletries out the window onto the sidewalk. She stood out there a long while, trying to pack her stuff and cursing at anyone who had the misfortune to walk by.

I never saw her again, but someone told me that she died of cancer before her 35th birthday.

I flew down to Florida the next morning, but my dad had already been cremated. That evening, there was a memorial service for him, and I was asked to give the eulogy. I got up to speak but couldn't get the words out clearly. I was so high on heroin that I could barely stand up. I was helped off the podium, and everyone thought that I was so distraught by the death of my father that I couldn't even stand straight. But the truth was that I almost didn't know where I was.

Heroin was taking over my life. It wouldn't be long before I hit the bottom.

Back home, one of the photographers with whom I worked was shooting a very big campaign for a large, well-known clothing manufacturer. I was booked on the job and flew to the Caribbean where it was being shot.

The model was on board a very large yacht that just sailed back and forth about 100 yards off shore. The model and I were the only people on board. My job was to stay hidden underneath, in the cabin, and only come up to wipe the sweat off him every once in a while. (I was being paid $3,000 a day to do this!)

Three platforms were built on the beach. The center platform had the master camera. This was where the director was seated with a TV monitor to watch and direct the shooting.

The side platforms had two other cameras set up on them. In addition to these three cameras on the shore, a helicopter with a film crew on board had a cameraman strapped to the side of the copter. They were to fly over the sailboat, swooping down for aerial shots. Yet another film crew was strapped into a motorboat that was to circle us every few minutes. It was a piece of cake job, but I was bored.

Down below and alone, I decided to go into the bathroom and shoot a bag of dope. I locked the teak door and pulled out my syringe works. I cooked the heroin in a spoon and drew up the liquid into the syringe. I then injected myself.

Suddenly, as I felt the drug make its way through my body, I realized that I had shot too much. But it was too late. I was drifting into unconsciousness and couldn't fight it. The darkness closed in on me and I dropped to the floor in an overdose.

When I didn't come up to take care of the model, all production stopped. The crew forced the door open and the Coast Guard was called. The Coast Guard revived me.

The client was, needless to say, furious. I was sent back to New York, and someone else was called in to replace me and finish the job. I had crossed an invisible line. I was now considered an insurance risk. At that level of the business, no matter how hard you try to keep your addiction quiet, you can't. Word got out that I had become unreliable. Funny enough, I actually had clients who supplied the drugs, having them ready and waiting for me when I arrived on the job. These very clients now turned their backs on me. I even had one client who would pick me up by limousine, and the driver had several $100 dollar bills for me. He drove me to buy drugs, and then took me to the studio. But now, with such a public overdose, all bets were off.

Clients began to pull away like rats on a sinking ship. They cancelled all of my future bookings, and I was being more or less blackballed. Not surprisingly, my career nosedived. Life began to crumble all around me, and I didn't even care. It was too much to think about. All I wanted to do was shoot dope. I would lay all alone in my 5,000 square-foot loft, shoot enough heroin to pass out for eight or 10 hours, wake up, and shoot some more.

I would eat only occasionally by ordering in some food. I would leave the apartment only when my supply of drugs ran out and I had to buy more.

My phone rang constantly. Creditors called wanting payment. Accountants rang to discuss the sorry state of my accounts. Lawyers called with threats. I knew it was just a matter of time before the police would come to lock the loft to keep me out.

I went into another rehab. This was a last-resort effort to give it one more shot. I had been in about six rehabs already—some were 30-day programs, but most were only for long weekends or a few days. None of them ever worked, and neither did this latest one. As a matter of fact, on my way home from the rehab facility, I got out of the cab and bought more drugs.

My life was in shambles, but all I wanted to do was shoot dope. Nothing else mattered or had any meaning. I couldn't fight anymore. I was lost and hopeless. There seemed to be no way out.

Finally, I completely abandoned myself to my situation. All hope was gone. *Once a dope fiend, always a dope fiend,* I thought to myself.

I got out of bed, walked into the living room, lit a cigarette, sat down, and looked around. I thought about selling all of my beautiful furniture, piece by piece. That would certainly bring in the money to pay off my bills, but it seemed like too much of an effort for me. I would have to call dealers, then the buyers would want to see the pieces, and offers would be made. I decided it was too much to think about. It wouldn't help anyway. It would only scratch the surface of what I owed.

I couldn't even cry. I had reached a point of total acceptance of my situation and I wasn't strong enough to change it. I thought about how nice it would be if someone would come along, reach out to me, and say, "I will help you." If only there was someone who would take me by the hand and show me the way out. If only someone could change me, change who I was deep inside. If only someone could show me how to fill the emptiness I had always felt.

But all this seemed like a mere fantasy. There was nobody who could fill that void for me. I was all alone.

I knew now what I had to do. I sat in one of my beautiful chairs, pulled a garbage can between my legs, and began to cut up anything that had my name on it. I cut up my driver's license, my passport, leases, contracts, invoices, bills ... anything that could be attributed to me.

I then dressed as warmly as I could, put the keys to the loft on a table, and walked out of the apartment. I let the door close and lock behind me as I walked out into the streets of New York City. I knew that I would never come back.

I had nowhere to go, no ID on me, and no money. I was officially homeless, and all I wanted to do was shoot dope.

CHAPTER 9

Life on the Streets

Then I realized that God allows people to continue in their
sinful ways so he can test them. That way, they can see
for themselves that they are no better than animals.
ECCLESIASTES 3:18

I spent most of my first night on the street just walking around the Lower East Side. All the days of my life seemed to be running through my head.

I remembered my childhood.

I remembered my friends from school.

I remembered coming to New York.

I thought about my ex-wife and wondered where she was.

I remembered my days of shopping in Paris and of cruising the beaches of Saint-Tropez.

I wondered what would happen with my family. Would they look for me? When would they give up looking for me? Would they wonder if I was dead?

I thought about how my nieces would grow up. Who would they marry?

I remembered Toni and wondered if she was better off now.

I remembered everything, but felt nothing.

I thought about all the things I should have done differently when I had the chance. All those rehabs I had checked into and how I had gotten high within an hour of leaving them.

I once had it all, but what did it matter now? The empty hole in the center of my soul was never satisfied. It was even deeper and emptier now.

What would I do? Where would I go? Who would ever help me?

My loneliness was so deep that I couldn't let my mind explore it. If I looked at it, it threatened to consume me. I needed desperately to buy some drugs, but how would I get the money? What would I have to do in the streets for the money?

I know that it will seem strange to hear this, but even though this was the most devastating experience that had ever happened to me, at the same time, it was as if a big burden had been lifted off me.

I didn't have to pretend any more.

I didn't have to pretend that I was someone that I wasn't.

I didn't have to pretend that I had it all together anymore.

Most of my life, I had felt that I was bluffing. I felt that everyone else knew what life was all about, but I didn't. I felt that everyone else had the answer to the mystery of life, but I was out in the dark somehow. I felt that everyone knew how to be happy, except me. I had all the things that I thought should have made me happy, and I still was miserable.

I had been in the inner circle of things that I thought would make my life full and satisfying, and I still was lonely. I felt that I had no one to talk to, and whenever I did try to talk to someone, I felt that I was not understood.

Why were other people so happy? What did it take? I just couldn't understand it.

Finally giving up on life was somehow satisfying, in a strange and twisted way.

Now, I had to do whatever was necessary to make money, but the struggle to succeed and be someone I wasn't was over.

Homeless and desperate, I decided to do whatever I had to do to earn enough money to get by—enough money to keep me in drugs and keep me numb enough not to care about anything else.

I noticed some guys standing on the corner. They were not from the neighborhood and looked a little nervous. I saw some potential for making money.

"Need some help copping some good dope?" I asked, as I passed them.

"Yeah, dude! Who's got the good stuff?"

"I can take you where the good dope is but what's in it for me?" I asked.

"We'll throw you a couples of bags, dude!"

They didn't have to ask me twice.

"Let's go!" I said.

They bought the drugs, and I got paid in heroin. We agreed to meet at the same spot every day, at around the same time. I began to walk around the neighborhood, looking for these types of opportunities to score a few bags of dope.

It was probably two or three in the morning, and I was dog-tired. It started to rain. *What would I do now?* I wondered. I stood in a doorway for a long time, just staring out into the dark and rainy night.

I looked up at the buildings and watched as lights would turn off in apartments. People were turning in for the night.

As it got later and later, I began to walk again. I had to find shelter of some kind and go to sleep. My stomach ached from hunger. How did people on the streets eat? Would I have to scavenge in dumpsters behind restaurants for thrown-out food? Would I have to fight off the rats for a meal?

In the distance, I could see a cardboard box about the size of a large TV. I pulled out the junk that was in the box and crawled in. I slept almost immediately.

When I woke up, it was daylight and the sun had come out. People hurried by, rushing to catch buses and trains on their way to work.

No one made eye contact with me. Making eye contact might mean that you would be asked for money. Savvy New Yorkers have a way of seeing everything out of a peripheral vision, so as to stay aware of any possible danger in their immediate surroundings. They never look directly at anything.

With nowhere to go, I just began to walk aimlessly.

Life on the streets centered on looking for money to buy drugs, buying the drugs, and then finding somewhere to shoot the drugs. This usually took place in an abandoned building or on the rooftop of some unlocked building.

One day, I met a guy while I was buying drugs, and he asked me where I was going to go to shoot up.

"I'm not sure," I answered.

"I have a place to go," he said. "You can come with me."

We walked further downtown and came to the Brooklyn Bridge on the Manhattan side. Under the bridge was a series of archways with huge wooden doors that had been closed up by the city. They were chained and padlocked from the outside.

This guy walked up to one of the sets of doors and knocked a code. I heard bolts slide, and one of the doors cracked open just enough to let us enter. Inside were three Asian men.

"This is my friend, Danny," my new found friend introduced me.

They nodded their heads and went about their business. I looked around—piles of junk and garbage everywhere. Two of the Chinese men had their own space cleared away, and makeshift beds were set up with some personal items stored in boxes beside each bed.

My new friend walked up to some sheets of industrial plastic that hung in one corner of the area to separate it from the rest of the space. He lifted away one side of the plastic, slipped inside, and held it open for me.

"Come on in," he said.

I ducked my head and slipped into the area. Inside the area enclosed by the plastic, the space was warm. A large king-size mattress was on the floor, with blankets neatly tucked around the edges. There was a heater blazing in one corner and a television in another. He picked up a remote and turned on the TV. I started laughing.

"How do you get electricity?" I asked.

"I tapped into the electricity from the bridge."

There was even a desk with a chair, a table with a hot plate on it, and a recliner in the "room."

"So, this is your space, huh? And who are these Chinese guys?" I asked.

"The shorter guy is the leader of the Shadow Dragons street gang. He's in hiding. He's wanted for gun smuggling, drug smuggling, and seven murders. The other two are his slaves."

"Oh!" was all I could say. The Shadow Dragons was one of the most violent of the Chinese gangs. I noticed that lots of cats roamed around this space.

"Are the cats for food?" I joked.

He laughed and said, "No, they keep the large rats under control."

Again, all I could say was, "Oh!"

This sure was a far cry from my luxurious loft, but it was better than sleeping in a carton box.

I lived in this space under the Brooklyn Bridge with my friend for the next couple of weeks. His name, by the way, was Lucky!

I learned the door knock code, and there was always someone inside to let me enter.

Lucky and I shared our drugs. If he scored big on any given day, he shared with me. When I scored, I shared with him.

The Chinese men mostly kept to themselves and respected our privacy, probably because Lucky was the first one to find the place and set it up. He had taken in the Asian men and provided a shelter where they could hide from the police. They often had Chinese food delivered to them from some friend in Chinatown and would give us whatever we wanted to eat.

The cats weren't fed so that they would be better hunters of the very large rats. These rats seemed to scurry by so quickly we weren't even sure we saw them.

I arrived back at our shelter one day to find the chain and lock on the outside of the doors busted and hanging. The doors were slightly open.

This was not the norm. Something was very wrong. I pushed the door open a little more and a feeling of fear swept over me. The inside bolts had been forced open and torn from the wood. I stuck my head in and looked around. I saw no dead bodies so I decided to go enter.

The "slaves'" beds were overturned, all of their belongings were scattered around, and looked like they had been stomped into the ground. I stepped in cautiously.

Everything was dark except for the little light that came from the outside. Very carefully, I walked to Lucky's area. The sheet of plastic was ripped down. Everything was overturned. Wires were pulled and hanging. The TV was smashed.

I knew that I had to get out of there as quickly as possible. Fear gripped me hard, and I ran as far from there as I could go. I never saw any of these people again.

I was alone on the streets once again, and my life consisted of making money where I could and sleeping where I could, and, of course, the drugs.

Every once in a while, I would go to a pay phone and call my agent collect. She had become a friend, and it was a familiar voice on the other side of the line. She would ask me how I was.

"Okay," I said.

She would then tell me that my brother and sister-in-law called often to see if she had heard from me. "Call them; they worry about you," she urged.

I knew that I wouldn't call. I didn't want them to see me like this.

One day, my agent told me that a model from the Ford Agency had called asking about me. Her name was Wanda and she had left a number.

It's that religious fanatic, I thought.

"She said she could use a good haircut, and you could come to her house. She would pay you in cash to cut her and her roommate's hair."

I took Wanda's number and called her. At least I could make some money. That was my incentive. Wanda was very sweet on the phone. She said I could come over whenever I wanted.

I made arrangements to go to Brooklyn that evening. All I had to do was steal a pair of scissors and a comb. I shoplifted them from a local drug store, jumped the turnstile in the subway, and went to Brooklyn.

I was a mess, but Wanda pretended not to notice. I began to cut hair while she and her roommate, Liz, talked about the Lord and even played a videotape of the Brooklyn Tabernacle Choir in concert for me to watch. On the video, there was a testimonial by a guy named Calvin Hunt. He related how crack had caused him to leave his family and live in the streets. He was actually living in a doghouse in Queens, NY. Somehow, he said, God rescued him, and now he sang in his church.

After he spoke, he sang a song called *I'm Clean*. It touched me because the guy seemed so sincere. I felt so detached from the world, but this man had something that I wanted—inner peace. He didn't have to do drugs anymore.

Before I left, Wanda and Liz both took my hands and prayed for me. I was beginning to get sick from the lack of drugs. I wanted to get out of there. But, suddenly and inexplicably, I turned around and walked back to the living room, and sat down in a chair.

"My life is a mess and I don't know what to do," I said.

Maybe Calvin's story had made me a bit vulnerable. I really don't know.

Liz pulled a chair up to me and asked what was it like for me, what was I feeling?

I told her that I felt as though I was lost in a dense forest. I used to be able to come and go as I pleased. But now I had gone in so deeply, that I couldn't find my way out anymore. It was very dark in there. No light could penetrate through the treetops. I was lost and didn't know which way was out. I seemed to be groping in the darkness. Suddenly, Liz burst into tears and began to sob. I got so freaked that I got up and ran out of the apartment.

Soon, Liz got in touch with me through my agent and told me that her Youth Choir was going to be singing at a church on the Lower East Side, and she wanted me to come. She gave me the address. I knew the location well, but didn't recall ever seeing a church there. I only knew of an after-hours nightclub on that block that was notorious for drugs. The bouncers knew who the local drug addicts were and would let us in free. We could buy drugs by the bar, and go up into the balcony to shoot them.

I took the address that Liz had given me and the following Sunday went looking for the church. To my surprise, the club was not a club anymore; it was now a church! They had purchased the building and renovated it. This was where the Youth Choir was going to be performing. I thought it was funny.

I stepped into the main entrance, was welcomed, and handed a bulletin. Then the usher pointed towards the main sanctuary. I walked into the sanctuary and decided that I didn't want to sit with other people, but preferred to stand in the back of the church, leaning against the wall.

A few minutes later, a man walked up to me and introduced himself as the pastor. He asked if he could get me a seat. I told him that I preferred to stand.

He tried again, this time saying that he had a special seat right up front just for me. Again, I said no. When he tried a third time to get me to sit down, I got an attitude and walked right out of the church.

Why couldn't they just leave me alone? I thought. *These Christians were so annoying: Always being so nice. What was up with them anyway?*

Back on the street, I looked for any opportunity to make a buck. I observed people and became pretty good at figuring out why they did what they did. I naturally gravitated to those people who were the strongest in the street. I also knew they were the strongest, because they were the most feared.

People had always been protective of me for some reason, and this hadn't changed in this subculture. Not only did I gravitate to the strongest people, but I also had the ability to submit to these people's authority. It was a matter of survival.

People began to know me on the streets. They began to trust me. They could give me large amounts of money or drugs to move from one location to another. I knew that if I messed up, I was a dead man. I also knew that if I didn't mess up, I would earn the drugs I needed, and it also set me up for future "work."

The only contact I still maintained with my former life was my agent. I called her regularly. Always the same questions, always the same people who called.

I never returned my brother and sister-in-law's calls, though I knew they were concerned about me. I always told them I was living with a friend, but they suspected I had been homeless. The last time I had seen my family had been very hard on David.

Every Christmas Eve, I would try to pull myself together and catch a bus to Pennsylvania to spend the holidays with David, his wife Cynthia, and their two little girls. I looked forward to seeing my nieces open their gifts.

In their home on Christmas morning in 1994, I went to the bathroom to shoot drugs. I must have been in there long enough to arouse David's and Cynthia's suspicions, because they started to knock on the door, asking whether I was okay. When I opened the door, it became clear to them that I was anything but okay. I was, needless to say, under the influence of drugs, could barely walk or talk, and was too far gone to realize how abusive this behavior was toward David, Cynthia, and, most especially, my little nieces. As soon as I became somewhat coherent, David told me to pack by bags; he was taking me to the bus station.

When he dropped me off at the station, he handed me the pictures of my nieces stapled into a Ziploc bag. He embraced me long and hard, not letting me pull away as his body heaved with sobs. He whispered in my ear, "Keep these pictures on you, and remember your nieces this way, but don't ever come back to visit. I'll tell them what a good uncle you were, and what a great big brother you were to me. But I don't want the girls to find you dead in the bathroom, or to remember you like this." Then he released me, turned, and walked away without looking back.

He was right. I also didn't want my nieces, who were very young at that time, to have those kinds of memories of me. They would remember me through pictures and happy stories my brother would tell them.

I called Wanda in hopes of making some more money, but it wasn't a haircut she needed. Her choir was going to perform at Radio City Music Hall. She had a ticket for me and wanted me to come.

How could I go to Radio City Music Hall? I was a homeless drug addict. Even if I wanted to go, I had nothing to wear. Wanda said she could buy me some clothes. She was so persistent that I finally agreed to go.

I showed up that night for the concert, even though I was a bit disheveled and probably didn't smell the greatest. I had a ticket in my hand and got to my seat with no problem.

The concert started, and the choir sang so beautifully that I thought this must be what heaven was like. At the end of the concert, the pastor came out and spoke. His words were engaging, and when he asked those who were looking for a second chance at life to stand, I got up.

Deep inside, I knew that I couldn't keep on living this way. I was in really bad shape. I had nothing left to live for—no job, no family, no money, no real friends. I was seriously ill, having contracted hepatitis many years earlier. Now that I was using so much, my side was swollen and my liver ached.

Then the pastor called all those standing to come forward to the front of the auditorium. That's when I sat back down. No way was I walking up in front of all these people. Later, I left the concert hall and headed back downtown.

I thought of everything I had heard that evening. What was I thinking? How could walking to the front of the audience at Radio City Music Hall help me in any way at all? It was just more of that religious fantasy.

CHAPTER 10

Life Gets Worse But I
Hear Good News

The words of the wise are more to be heeded
than the shouts of a ruler of fools.
ECCLESIASTES 9:17

I had a friend with whom I used to get high, but who was now clean. He lived on the Lower East Side, right in the middle of all the drug dealing. How he managed to get clean, I don't know. He saw me on the streets one day and asked me to come over, so he could try to help me.

I couldn't believe my luck. He lived by himself and had two bedrooms. He let me stay in the second bedroom. The next few months were certainly easier. It was winter, and at least I had some shelter from the freezing cold.

I started going with him to Alcoholic Anonymous, Narcotics Anonymous, as well as other groups for addicts. *This is how he stays clean,* I thought. *Going from meeting to meeting doesn't leave him time for anything else.*

I listened carefully as one person after another talked about how they wanted to "use" but were working their "steps." Half the people there seemed to be coming back after a binge. "Welcome back!" the whole group would chant.

I, however, never stopped using.

One day, my friend announced that he was moving out of the apartment to a nicer one in a better neighborhood. He said he didn't want me to come with him because I couldn't get on with the program. He told me that I could stay in this apartment until the lease was up, but I would be responsible for the rent.

I needed to make some money fast so I wouldn't be homeless. I talked to the local drug dealer and told him I wanted to sell for him. He agreed. I began to deal in front of the building across the street from where I was living.

The dealer stayed upstairs with his hooker girlfriend and doled out five bundles of dope to each of his sellers at a time. I would go downstairs, sell the five bundles, bring the money upstairs, and take five more bundles.

I was able to pay the rent and get high too.

A few weeks after I started selling on the street, I was promoted to staying upstairs, handing out the bundles, and collecting the money. He watched TV and nodded off in a recliner. His girlfriend never left the bed.

The lease on my apartment was coming to an end and I would have to leave. I had turned the apartment into a shooting gallery, and a place where the local hookers could bring their tricks at any hour of the day or night.

I got paid each time they used the apartment. There was a mattress on the floor in the second bedroom and they could use the bathroom to wash up after each trick. Money-wise, that was a good set-up, but soon I would have to give it up. I had to find another arrangement.

One day, as my drug dealer boss slept in the recliner, I walked out of the apartment with all the drugs and all the money. I don't know why I did it, but I remember that I wasn't scared, probably because drugs numb feelings, as well as any sense of right and wrong. I still had the awareness that this kind of betrayal could cost me my life. I knew I had to get out of the neighborhood right away.

Addicts and dealers never venture outside of a five or six block area that constitutes their turf. I could disappear into another neighborhood and not be found.

I never returned to that apartment. I got on a subway as fast as I could, got out of the Lower East Side, and headed up to Harlem. If I stayed around the Lower East Side now, I wouldn't live through the night.

I knew my way around Harlem well enough. I had been there many times to buy drugs when the drugs on the Lower East Side had dried up because of police raids. I had enough money and drugs on me to get by for a few days.

That first night, I walked around Harlem, getting a feel for what went on in that area. I never stopped to think that a white man walking the streets of Harlem in the middle of the night might be a sitting duck.

Fear was not in my vocabulary. The only thing I knew was survival. I quickly found out where the all-night dealers were. I found out who sold heroin, who sold coke, and who sold crack.

I also saw where the hookers congregated on Park Avenue and 120th Street, half naked, even in the freezing cold. Men would drive around as the girls looked in and waved or threw kisses. I sat for a long time on a short wall near the stroll and watched all the action.

A young Puerto Rican guy walked by and stopped. He was a bit hesitant at first, and I knew that he was being cautious in case I was a cop or an informant. Then he took his chance. He asked me if he could help me buy drugs.

My old job, I thought. I said no. I had drugs, but I had nowhere to go. He invited me to come up to his mother's apartment in one of the government-subsidized buildings on Second Avenue.

"Sure, let's go," I said.

His mother's apartment was a large studio. One big room with a walk-in closet, a small bathroom, and kitchen. It was so roach-infested that the roaches even walked upside down on the ceiling. The place stunk.

The mother had mental problems and talked in an incoherent gibberish. She just walked around the room aimlessly. I was told she often walked right out of the apartment, not closing the door behind her, and disappeared for hours. She would also lie for a long time on her twin mattress on the floor, staring up at the ceiling and mumbling incoherently.

My new friend, Shorty, an affectionate nickname given to just about any short Puerto Rican male or female, slept in the walk-in closet on a pile of dirty clothes. That's where I slept for the next couple of months as well.

Little by little, I met other addicts who lived in the building and managed to get the money for drugs every day one way or another. There were all kinds of new scams in Harlem to make money.

One couple I met let me tag along with them on their daily shoplifting sprees. They would go into record stores and, while the man would act very suspiciously and get all the employees' attention thinking he was a shoplifter, the woman would rob them blind. Once she was out of the store, the man would put down everything he had managed to pick up and walk out too.

Then they would go to their fence—a person who would buy the stolen merchandise from them and resell it to someone else. He would give them $5 for each popular CD, and we would go off to buy drugs.

I learned to be one of the decoy distracters. I would enter the store after they were already inside and position myself between the store employees and the shoplifter. I would lean over in a way that totally blocked their view. She was so fast that she would manage to get dozens of CDs under her skirt and hold them all between her legs as she walked casually out of the store. She had some kind of rig under her skirt strapped around her waist with a bag of some sort hanging between her legs. She was proud of her invention and bragged about how much money she could make if she advertised and sold this gadget to other shoplifters.

She ended up going to jail for 10 years on grand larceny charges, while her man just disappeared somewhere into the underworld. No one knows what happened to him. As for me, I walked away from it all.

One day I bought two bags of dope and went into an empty condemned building to shoot them. Two young African-American boys also came into the building to shoot what they had bought from the same dealer. They had to be 18 or 19 years old.

I was having trouble getting my needle into a vein. My veins were collapsing and finding a vein was getting harder and harder. The two young guys both hit a vein almost immediately. They pushed the plungers on their syringes and 15 seconds later they both dropped to the floor. They were dead. I immediately pulled the needle out of my arm without shooting the dope, threw the syringe on the dirt floor, and left the building.

A while later, the place was swarming with police. Ambulances pulled up and took the two boys away. I later found out that we had been sold rat poison.

Another time, I was shooting dope in another abandoned building A young guy came in and put a gun to my forehead.

"Give me all your money!" he demanded.

I started laughing. "What money? Why are you robbing a homeless drug addict? Isn't that kind of stupid? Go rob someone in midtown, who actually has money. I don't have anything."

He got crazy. "I said, give me all your money or I'll blow your brains out," he yelled.

"I told you that I don't have any money. But do me a favor. Blow my brains out. Please put me out of my misery!" I pressed my forehead hard against the barrel of his gun.

Suddenly, he lowered his gun and backed away from me. "You're crazy, bro! You're crazy!" he said. He backed up all the way out of the building.

"Punk!" I yelled. How dare he come in here and try to rob me. To make money, I began to run drugs for the hookers. They had seen me around enough and knew I didn't befriend them for sex.

Most of these girls worked independently. They didn't all have pimps, but all had drug habits. They would turn a trick, jump out of the car, and look around for me. They gave me money to go buy them dope. I would go to "cop" (buy) the drugs and they would jump into another car. When they got back, I would give them their drugs. They would pay me with a bag, hand me more money, and I would do another run.

The girls trusted me and I never let them down. They worked hard for their money, like the song says. I felt sorry for them, but I wasn't in any shape to help them in any way.

One of the hookers in particular was always very nice to me. Sometimes we would talk for hours while getting high somewhere. She was a gypsy and lived in Hoboken, New Jersey. Her name was Christy. She was getting older. She told me how she longed to quit the game and get her life straight. She said she could read palms and wanted to someday open a small business helping people by telling them their futures. She was very lost. Even though she broke my heart when she talked to me about her dreams, I would try to encourage her.

When I earned enough drugs, I would return to the apartment with Shorty and my closet bedroom. Christy would go back to the stroll. I looked for her every day.

I had met another woman named Yolanda, who lived in the same building as Shorty. She didn't touch heroin, but loved to smoke crack. She had been a model in her youth. Once in a while, Yolanda would get high, pull out her old portfolio of modeling pictures, and reminisce about the old days before crack had taken its grip on her. She told me she had had a boyfriend who sang jingles for TV commercials. Together, they had made a lot of money but got messed up on crack. Her now ex-boyfriend was living in a subway tunnel somewhere in Manhattan. She would sit for a long time with her portfolio on her lap, staring into some place in her mind and remembering all the days she would never see again.

Yolanda taught me to cook her cocaine down into "base" — crack without the chemicals. She told me she could hook me up with dealers who paid $200 for a "cooker," someone who could cook large amounts of cocaine down into base to be mixed with chemicals and sold for crack. I told her I would give it a try. She made a phone call.

Later that same night, a very scary looking man arrived at her apartment.

"You the cooker?" he asked, as he looked me up and down.

"Yeah," I answered.

He pulled out about a pound of cocaine and handed it to me. Then he pulled out a gun and laid it on the kitchen counter.

"You mess up my coke and I'll shoot you," he said.

I picked up the glass coffee pot from a Mr. Coffee machine. I had never cooked that much coke before. I put the entire pound in the coffee pot, added water, and a teaspoon of baking soda.

I lit the stove and began to cook the cocaine. I was pretty nervous, even with all the drugs in my system. If this coffee pot were to burst because of the flames from the gas stove, I was a dead man.

I held the pot over the flames a few seconds and swirled the mixture. I kept holding it over the open flame for a couple of seconds at a time, pulling away and swirling. Like a scientist concocting potions in his lab, I was being very careful and very focused. Slowly, I tapped in more baking soda. More flames, more swirling. All the while this man was looking over my shoulder.

The mixture in the pot turned suddenly into a large oil ball that floated to the top of the water. I moved to the sink and ran a little tepid water into the pot. The oil ball began to solidify. I slowly added colder and colder water. The ball hardened completely. I wasn't going to get shot after all. I reached into the pot, pulled out a ball of "free base" about the size of a fist, and laid it on a plate.

"There you are," I said, with a sudden cocky confidence.

"That's the first time I ever saw someone cook the entire thing at once. And you wasn't even afraid!" the gun-toting hoodlum said, with obvious amazement in his voice.

He picked up the hard ball of base and put it into a zip lock bag, pulled out two $100 bills, and put his gun away.

"I'll tell the boys you are the best cooker in Harlem, even if you are white," he said.

However, I decided right there and then to retire from the cooking business. I was living dangerously enough as it was. When he walked out the door, my knees really began to knock and I had to sit down. My stomach was in a knot and I wanted to vomit.

With money in my pocket, I went out to buy a couple of bags of heroin and some cocaine for Yolanda. Drugs were so abundant and out in the open that finding them wasn't a hard job. You just had to look for the lines.

People would line up on the streets of Harlem, waiting to be served. Sometimes there were two lines. One was for people wanting just a few bags, and the other was an express line for people buying 10 bags or more. I stood in the second line.

There were about 20 people ahead of me. Suddenly, a large light blue Cadillac came barreling down the street and slammed its brakes right next to my line. Three men jumped out of the car with guns drawn and shot 10 or 12 bullets into the guy standing right in front of me.

Everyone began to scream and run in every direction. The guy who was shot slumped to the sidewalk. Smoke seemed to come out of the bullet holes all over his body, and a black pool of blood began to form around him. The three men jumped back into the car and sped away.

My eyes darted around, looking for the dealer. I saw that he was halfway down the block, running like everyone else. I jumped over the man who had been shot and ran as fast as I could. I caught up with the dealer and said, "Here's a hundred dollar bill. Hand me a bundle!"

"Are you crazy? Run!"

"Hand me a bundle!" I yelled again, holding out the bill.

Still running at full speed, he grabbed the bill and handed me a bundle of dope. I stopped running, casually turned the corner, and walked as if nothing had happened. I walked around the block to Yolanda's apartment.

From the 20th floor, I looked down at the crime scene. Police had blocked off the street and were doing whatever they do when they arrive at a murder scene. The next morning, the activity on the street showed no indication that anything had happened the night before. That was what an average day on the street was like—always living on the edge, never knowing what tomorrow would bring, and if you would still be alive.

One night, I arrived home to find Shorty lying face down on the floor of our closet. There was lots of blood. He had been shot by a stray bullet. It had caught him in the right upper thigh, from the back.

He was weak as I turned him over. I told him that I was calling an ambulance. He insisted that he didn't want to go to the hospital because they would involve the police. I saw that there was an exit hole in the front of his pants. I undid his pants and pulled them down. He screamed in pain.

The wounds had dried and stopped bleeding. That was a good sign. It meant that the bullet hadn't hit any major vein or artery. I went to the drugstore and bought whatever I thought might help: gauze, peroxide, swabs, anti-bacterial cream, and iodine. I came back to the closet and cleaned Shorty's wound both front and back with alcohol and peroxide. I applied globs of anti-bacterial cream and wrapped his leg with gauze and surgical tape. I kept tabs on him all night and he seemed to sleep fine except for a slight fever.

The next day, he seemed alert and rested. I redressed the wounds and, over the next few days he was up and walking around. No infection—that was what I worried about more than anything else.

Word got out on the street about what I had done. Everyone began to call me "Doctor." People started to come to me with abscesses and all kinds of weird things. I would do what I could. I would clean out the infections from abscesses and dress the wounds. They would heal and tell everyone that the "Doctor" took care of them.

Sometimes they needed further antibiotics and would go to emergency rooms to get them. One woman told me that when a real doctor at a local emergency room looked at her wound, he commented on what a good job the previous doctor had done in cleaning and dressing the wound. We had a good laugh about that.

It had been a long time since I had called my agent. I decided to check in and let her know that I was still alive. She told me that my family still called often, asking her if she had heard from me. She also said that the model from Ford, Wanda, continued to call. Wanda had told her that I could phone her anytime because she, Liz, and several other friends of hers could all use haircuts. I couldn't believe that she still called or, for that matter, cared.

I called Wanda. She said she could get a few of her friends over to her apartment in Brooklyn, and I could make some money.

I asked her when she wanted to do this. She said, "What about tomorrow, Saturday?"

I said I would come over on Saturday afternoon. I asked if I could meet her that night, and if she could advance me part of the money. She thought for a minute and agreed, but it was Friday evening and she was on her way to choir practice at her church. I would have to come by the church to pick up the money. I got the address, jumped the turnstile in the subway, and headed to her church in Brooklyn.

When I arrived at the church on Flatbush Avenue, I walked up to the reception desk.

"I'm here to see Wanda Geddie," I told the girl at the desk.

"Sure, I'll get her. Have a seat. Can I get you a cup of coffee?" she asked.

Why were these Christians so nice? It was like they were programmed or something. I mean, why was everyone so happy, always smiling? It was so strange to me.

Wanda came out with a big smile (of course) and had another girl with her.

"This is my friend, Roberta. I wanted you to meet her. She went through the same stuff you are going through now."

Roberta smiled (of course) and said hello. I looked her over. I decided that there was no way she ever went through anything even remotely resembling what I was going through. She looked too good.

Roberta sat down next to me. She told me that she had been an intravenous heroin addict and also smoked crack. She said God had rescued her from this lifestyle, and now she ran an outreach ministry here in the church. She invited me to come sometime.

I found it hard to believe but listened with semi-interest.

Wanda then told me that one of her pastors wanted to pray with me. She led me to his office, the four of us joined hands, and they all prayed. I remember looking up with one eye open at the three of them. They were so into this. They really believed in this praying stuff. *Unbelievable,* I thought. *Oh well, whatever floats your boat!* When they finished praying, the girls left the office and the pastor asked me to sit down.

He talked to me for a while about Jesus. He said that the church was prepared to help me get into a Christian rehabilitation facility.

"No thanks," I quickly said. "I'm not interested."

"Well, if you ever change your mind, you know we are here," he answered with a smile (of course).

When I came out of the office, Wanda was waiting for me in the reception area. In her hand, she held a Bible. She handed it to me and said, "Here, I want you to have this Bible. Your money is somewhere inside. You'll find it."

When I got out of the church, I looked for the money and found it at the first page of the Book of John.

I jumped on the subway and headed back to Manhattan. I bought heroin with the money and sold the Bible to someone who told me his grandmother would like it. He gave me a pack of cigarettes and two new syringes for it.

The following day, I went to Wanda's apartment to cut everyone's hair— Wanda, Liz, and three other friends of hers.

When everyone's hair was cut, they paid me, and then they circled me. They all put a hand on me and began to pray. Oh man, I couldn't believe it—five of them at once! It was a Holy Ghost ambush.

As I was leaving, one of the friends, Damaris Carbaugh, said she was leaving also and would give me a ride back to Manhattan. We got into her car and headed over the Brooklyn Bridge. I had no idea at that point that Damaris was a very well-known Christian recording artist.

When we got into Manhattan, I told her that she could drop me off anywhere, and I would make my own way home.

"No," she said, "I'm going to take you right to your building!"

I was homeless. I had no building!

"Well then," I answered, "turn here and you can drop me off right in front of that little store on the corner. I want to pick up a few things before I go home."

When we stopped in front of the store, I thanked her for the ride and started to get out of the car. Damaris stopped me and asked if she could speak with me a minute. She told me a little about herself. As a teenager, she dreamt about becoming a famous singer in the secular world, but God had stopped her, and now she sang for the Lord. She said that it was the best decision she had ever made, and that Jesus had become her everything.

"Your EVERYTHING!" I said, mockingly.

"Yes, my everything. He's everything to me." She seemed unmoved by my mocking.

I repeated, incredulously, "Your *everything*?"

"Yes, my *everything*."

I got out of the car. *Whatever,* I thought. *These Christians are wacky.*

I ran down to the subway and jumped the turnstile heading to Harlem. I had to get out of the Lower East Side before someone saw me.

CHAPTER 11

From Death All Around Me to Life

*Anyone who is among the living has hope, even
a live dog is better off than a dead lion.*
ECCLESIASTES: 9:4

Christy, my gypsy hooker friend, and I used to get high, sit in some abandoned building, and talk, sometimes all night. Occasionally, I would go back to Hoboken with her and spend the night there.

Her room was in a cheap hotel, with a shower and toilet across the hall. She told me that she paid by the week. An elderly gentleman, who had an invalid wife, had been paying her rent there for many years. She would see him every Wednesday afternoon for an hour or so, and along with paying her rent, he would give her $300 a week to spend any way she wanted.

The only thing she wanted was heroin.

She had grown up in a family of gypsies who became rich by scamming people, promising to remove curses, and performing hex type rituals. They charged large sums of money for this "service."

Christy had somehow disgraced her family of con artists when they found out that she had a drug habit. Strange that robbing people was acceptable, but doing drugs was disgraceful. Her family cut her off financially and she began to prostitute herself on the streets.

She prided herself on the fact that she worked independently and had never had a pimp. That always seemed like a big deal to prostitutes. Pimps usually took all of the girls' money and treated them poorly. They usually had several girls working the streets. The pimps would give them drugs, but girls were never allowed to keep any of the money they earned. If the girls kept some of the money, they would be severely beaten in public, so that other hookers could see what happened to the ones who held out.

Christy had worked in a whorehouse for several years until the place was busted. Her Madam and many of the girls had been arrested. Somehow, she had gotten away.

Christy insisted that even though her family scammed people in the hexing and un-hexing business, she had a genuine gift of reading people's future in the palms of their hands. She told me that she wanted to use this gift to help people.

She was a good-hearted woman with the lowest self-esteem I had ever seen in anybody. She was also very lonely and always wanted me to stay with her. It was a welcome break for me from the monotony of walking the streets of Harlem or sleeping in Shorty's closet.

Christy always paid for all the drugs—and everything else, for that matter. She insisted on it. It was her way of keeping me around and also a way that she could express what a giving person she felt she was. At one point, I stayed with her for several months, but began go a little crazy in Christy's one room.

When we went to Manhattan every couple of days, she would hit the stroll and I would go visit Shorty, if I could find him.

Hoboken soon wore thin and I told Christy that I couldn't stay anymore. She said she was fine with me leaving, but I knew that she was trying hard to keep up a happy front. Tears filled her eyes, but she insisted that she wanted me to feel free to do what I wanted to do. She said she didn't want to hold me back.

Hold me back from what? I wondered.

I went back to Harlem and to the closet I shared with Shorty. Occasionally, I would see Christy on the stroll on Park Avenue and we would talk, but she had put up a cold wall. It was something that hookers seemed to be very good at. That was how they protected their hearts from being broken over and over again. Although she was always friendly toward me, it was never quite the same as before.

Sometime later, one of the other girls on the stroll told me that Christy had found a very large lump in her breast, but she refused to have it checked by a doctor. She was afraid that if she had to have her breast removed, she wouldn't be able to work anymore. She insisted that she would die with both breasts, no matter what. Her world had been reduced to one elderly man who paid the rent on her one room in a shabby hotel. It was a sad ending to an even sadder life. Soon after that, no one saw Christy on the street again. No one ever spoke of her.

Everybody living on the street had a nickname. No one's real identity was ever revealed. I was known as Danny, but nobody knew of the life I had once lived. I never mentioned to anyone the days of traveling the world with rock stars and working with famous models and designers. No one would have believed me anyway, and the less people knew about me, the better. All personal information could be turned against me someday, so like all street people, I was always cautious about revealing too many details.

For that reason, with the exception of Yolanda and Christy, I knew nothing about other people. I had no idea whether they had families, what work they used to do, or what dreams they'd once had. There were thousands of untold stories out there, including mine, but they were shrouded in secrecy and anonymity. Sometimes, I would catch someone at a vulnerable moment and get a glimpse of his or her life. But he or she would quickly clam up, realizing that maybe too much was said.

Yes, it was a lonely world on the streets. The word "friend" was used to describe someone you met or knew casually but not really in the deeper sense of trust and complicity. If your "friends" had to turn on you so that they could get by themselves, they would not hesitate to do it.

One such "friend" of mine was nicknamed Slim. He certainly lived up to his name. He was about 6'2 and rail thin. His government-subsidized apartment was a well-known shooting gallery.

On the first visit, we had to be brought by someone who was already "in," but after that we could always just show up at any time of the day or night and would be allowed to enter. We couldn't buy drugs there, but for $2 we could use a syringe from the many displayed in a coffee can on the table. All of them were pre-used. We would choose one, sharpen it on a book of matches, run some water through it, and use it.

We all knew about AIDS, but that didn't seem like a good enough reason not to use the syringes. Sometimes, we would get what was known on the street as a "bone crusher," some foreign object or substance that had gotten into the bloodstream. When that happened, we would shake and be in pain for a few minutes.

Slim had AIDS. Arthritis crippled his legs, arms, and hands. He couldn't handle a syringe and always needed someone to help him shoot his drugs. I volunteered often and was allowed to come in, use syringes, and stay all night, whenever I wanted. I was the "Doctor," after all.

One day, I showed up and Slim wasn't there. People in the apartment told me that he was taken by ambulance to a hospital, but they had no other information about him. I found someone who knew his real name and headed to Metropolitan Hospital to see if he was there. That was the usual hospital where everyone from my part of the city was taken.

When I got there and inquired about Slim, I was told that he was there. I was allowed to go up to his room. When I walked in, I won't ever forget the surprise on his face. He was so happy to see me and couldn't believe that someone would actually care enough to visit him. He looked pitiful lying in that bed. His long lanky limbs were twisted and crippled, and he was skinnier than ever. He asked me if I had any dope on me and I said yes, but no syringe.

I could fix that, though. I left the room for a minute. As I passed a rolling cart that was used by the nurses for dispensing drugs, I stole a syringe and went into a bathroom. I cooked up two bags of heroin and drew it up into the syringe. I put the cap back over the needle and hid it in my jacket. Back in Slim's room, I took out the syringe and injected the thin hose that went from the IV bag to the needle that was in his arm. A few minutes later, I saw the drugs do their job on him.

I returned to the hospital every day to inject Slim's IV. One day he told me that he was dying and wanted to spend his last days in his apartment. He asked me if I would check him out of the hospital. I told him that he wasn't mandated there by a court and could check himself out anytime he wanted.

I rang the bell for the nurse, and he informed her that he was leaving. I was already helping him into his clothes. The nurse called for a doctor, but we didn't stick around long enough. I walked Slim out the best I could and got us into a taxi.

When we got to Slim's apartment, I tied him off high up on his arm and injected him. When I pulled the needle out of his arm and was wiping him off, I accidentally jammed the bloody needle into the soft place between the thumb and forefinger of my left hand. Slim's face got very serious. He apologized over and over. He said that it was a death sentence.

I shrugged. "So what. I must have the virus already anyway. What difference does it make?" I no longer had the will to live.

Within a couple of days Slim died in his sleep.

✦

Seasons would come and go, but life didn't change much on the streets. Every day was a challenge. Every day was the same, and yet everyday was different. I had been homeless for several years at that point.

One day, as I was stepping off a curb to cross the street, a horrible fear suddenly gripped me. A wall had instantly materialized in front of me. It was an invisible wall, but to me it was real. I knew that I could pass through the wall, but I also sensed that if I did, something terrible would happen to me. A car would careen out of control and hit me, or someone would run up to me and stab me to death. This wasn't a rational fear, but there wasn't anything rational about my life.

I didn't know what exactly would happen, but only that something terrible *would* happen. I jumped back up on the curb and headed in the direction from where I had come. *What was all this about?* I wondered. *What had just happened to me?*

I was shaken by the incident.

A few days later, while walking on the sidewalk, it happened again. The invisible wall went up in front of me, and when I turned

MY DETOUR THROUGH HELL

to walk in the opposite direction, the wall went up again. I ran to the side and tried to go around "the wall."

This began to happen so frequently, that it began "dictating" where I could and couldn't walk. Sometimes, I would have to walk several blocks out of my way just to avoid crossing the imaginary wall. I was always aware that the walls could pop up anywhere, and could shift as they pleased.

No one could see these walls and I couldn't really see them either. I could only sense them, but they were very real and frightening to me. I began to walk around erratically, stopping and changing directions, suddenly crossing the street or walking flat up against a building because the "wall zone" was so close to my body.

Around this time, the voices began in my head, yelling, laughing, or mocking me. Tapes were always running over and over through my mind. I would think about what my life had become, and what I should have done differently.

I don't really know when those voices became independent of me or when I began to talk back to them. But I know that one day I realized that I was responding to voices that no one else could hear. These "conversations" went something like this:

"Why didn't I stay clean after that time I was away in rehab for 90 days? I was feeling so good."

"Because you didn't want to."

"Yes, I did. I just felt so empty inside, so lonely."

"That's because you're such a loser."

"I am not a loser. I had so much confidence at one time."

"You thought you did, but deep down you always knew what a loser you were. You aren't good for anything—never have been. You were born a loser and you'll die a loser!"

"Maybe you're right. I was always fearful deep inside."

"You know I'm right, you loser! Why don't you just die already! Just kill yourself. No one cares anyway. Nobody will ever miss you."

"I don't have the courage to kill myself."

"You see, you're such a loser, you can't even do that. You're a poor excuse for a human being! Just die!"

That kind of dialogue buzzed constantly in my head.

It began as just my voice in my head saying things like, "Why didn't I … I don't really know when it turned into … Because you're a … "

It was as if another person was speaking to me, and I was always defending myself against the accusations.

In addition, there was another voice that had been blurting out a steady stream of filthy words somewhere in the back of my mind. This voice was separate from the first voice and only spoke unconnected dirty words. It wasn't like, "You so-n-so." It was just individual curses, one after another. Soon both voices were competing in my mind for dominance and were joined by a third voice that just laughed incessantly and uncontrollably.

If you had stopped me on the street to ask me something, I could pull out of my "trance" and answer coherently. But as soon as I would walk away and be by myself, all the voices would start to wreak havoc in my head again.

By the way, hardly anyone ever stopped to talk to me. In fact, people probably crossed the street to get away from me, if they saw me coming. And who could blame them? I was like so many "crazy" people I see on the streets even today—looking disheveled, walking erratically, and talking out loud to unseen, unheard voices. Not exactly the kind of person with whom you engage in random conversations.

And as though these voices weren't bad enough, even more dysfunctions would materialize. For instance, when I would see a door that was slightly ajar, I would panic and not be able to move or to speak. The door could be closed and that was okay. It could be open and that was fine too. But when the door was slightly open, it was as if every muscle in my body refused to respond to my brain. If I tried to speak, I couldn't move my mouth and words wouldn't come out. I would stand this way for long periods of time, just staring at the half-opened door.

I was losing my mind and I felt that there was nothing I could do about it. I was very undernourished and at 5 feet 10 inches weighted about 108 pounds.

I was riding the trains all night, especially in the wintertime. The trains provided shelter from the cold, and if a police officer told me to get off, I would just catch another train.

One night, another addict, who was also riding the trains, came up and sat next to me. He asked me if I was okay. "You don't look so good," he said.

"You don't look so good yourself, bro," I answered.

"No, I mean you look *really* sick. You're completely yellow. You look like you're going to die. Listen, there is a hospital right above one of the stops coming up. You should go there."

Maybe I should go to the hospital, I thought. I didn't want to die on the streets. Who knows how long I would lie there before someone discovered that I was dead. No, this guy was right. I had to get to a hospital—not to try to get better, but to die there.

When the stop came up, the guy nodded to me that this was where I should get off. He asked if I wanted him to help me. I said that I could make it by myself. I was very thin and my side was a bit swollen from my liver. I had a lot of pain on the right side of my body. I walked a little hunched over to help relieve the pain.

When I came up from the subway, I saw the hospital across the street. I went up to the front entrance and it was locked. Hospitals in the Bronx are locked until five in the morning.

I sat on the sidewalk and leaned back against the building. The air was cold, but it felt good on my face, and I just huddled.

Waiting for the doors to open, I was sitting near a garbage bin and rats scurried back and forth. I didn't know which ones were real and which ones were imagined.

Sometimes, I imagined rats, thousands of rats. They crawled all over the place and all around me. Once, I broke through someone's wall with a bat because I imagined that a large breeder rat was behind the wall, breeding more rats by the hundreds. Sometimes, as the rats crawled around and the sun came up, they would begin to become transparent. In full sunlight, they would become invisible. I knew they were there, but no one else saw them. But this time my imagination wasn't playing tricks on me. These were real rats.

I weighed 108 pounds; my arms were covered with sores and abscesses. My shirtsleeves stuck to my arms. I was yellow with jaundice and voices screamed in my head. I had no ID on me, nothing that could identify me.

This is where I started this story.

As I sat there, I tried to focus. The voices kept accusing, cursing, and laughing. Some teenagers drinking beer walked by me. One kid put his thumb over the opening of his 40-ounce bottle and shook it. When the pressure built up, he pointed the bottle at me and squirted beer all over me. They all laughed and kept walking. At least they didn't beat me, kick me, or set me on fire, as had been done to other less fortunate homeless people.

The sky was getting a little brighter, even though it was still dark when the hospital finally unlocked the doors. I painfully stood up and in I walked.

The duty nurse took one look at me and called for assistance. She said I was completely yellow and should be admitted through emergency.

Attendants helped me to the ER. They brought me into an examination room and from then on things got hazy. I can't really remember with any clarity what happened there. Fear overwhelmed me. Some nurse kept slapping my face and asking me questions. Did I know where I was? Slap! Did I know what year it was? Slap! Stay with me, sir. Slap! How many fingers do I have held up? Slap!

Now, I might have been out of my mind, but I had enough sense not to slap someone in the face who had voices screaming in his head!

"Lady," I said, "You have two fingers in front of my face and, if you slap me again, I'm going to bite them both off!"

She jerked her hand away quickly and stopped the slapping.

This was it. I thought that I was close to the end. The altercation I was having with the nurse who kept slapping my face was annoying me. I didn't want to be annoyed just before dying.

I think I must have been injected with something that knocked me out, or maybe I slipped into unconsciousness all by myself, I don't know. The next thing I remember is waking up and lying naked on a hospital bed. I was confused.

I didn't immediately know where I was. But I could tell that I was in withdrawal, because I had vomited on myself. As soon as I began to come around, the voices in my head began to scream. The accusations, the filthy language, and the laughing took over my psyche. I wanted to pull my hair or bang my head against the headboard because, sometimes, if I could make myself feel pain, the voices didn't seem so loud.

I also wanted to jump out of bed and throw myself out of the window, but I could see that they were barred. Why couldn't I just die?

"Yes, you should die! You should kill yourself! Die! Die!" Loud laughing in my head was urging. "Kill Yourself! Die!"

Suddenly, in the midst of all the chaos and confusion going on in my head, for one moment there was silence. What happened next was truly mysterious. I don't know whether this was something I remembered Wanda saying, but I heard an angel whisper in my ear in a sweet little voice: "The day you call on the name of the Lord, He's going to set you free."

All too soon, the sweet voice was overpowered by the mocking and screaming voices. I knew that there was something I should remember, but what? My mind jumped around searching for the answer as the voices screamed.

Then again, for one instant, I heard that same soft voice whisper, "The day you call on the name of the Lord, He's going to set you free."

This time, I suddenly yelled out from somewhere deep inside of me, "JESUS! JESUS! HELP ME! OH GOD, HELP ME!"

I don't even remember everything I said, but I do remember thinking that maybe I needed a good referral since I didn't exactly live a saintly life, and maybe God wouldn't listen to my pleas. So I shouted, "Wanda told me that if I called on your name, you would set me free ... help me ... set me free!"

I will never forget that one moment because it was a turning point for me.

At that moment, it was as if the Spirit of the Living God swept into that hospital room and overwhelmed me.

At that moment, it was as if He was all around me, and inside of me.

At that moment, I knew that God was real and that He had heard me.

At that moment, I knew that He was touching me and healing me.

At that moment, I knew that God loved me.

At that moment, all the voices in my head stopped, and all my fears and phobias just disappeared.

I don't know how I knew, but I knew that I was in the presence of a Holy God.

Nothing about my situation had changed. I was still lying in my own vomit, but I knew at that moment I would never be the same again.

(1959) The last family photo before my Mom passed away from complications due to Lupus.

Father Johnny, Mother Elba, Younger Brother David & Me. I was 9 years old

BEAUTY SCHOOL DAYS: TAMPA, FLORIDA

In1967 I won the first of several First Place hairdressing competitions. I was 17 years old

MID 1980's : NEW YORK CITY

Dressed in my favorite tuxedo, living life in the fast lane

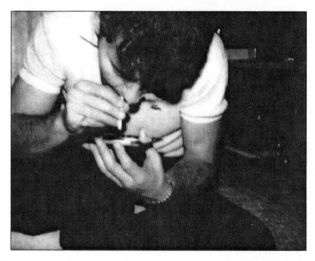

Cocaine was my drug of choice before I was introduced to Heroin

Late 1980's, High on the set of a photo shoot. Started losing weight.

Early 1990's, Looking gaunt had lost about 40 pounds

Early 1990's, Trying to look happy for my family as I hold my niece Bianca in a toy store.

Completely Stoned while working on a outdoor photo shoot. Note the brush in my hand and the hair-clips on my belt.

Leaning against a tree, trying not to fall, could hardly keep my eyes open...
While on the job!

Wanda's Wedding Day

I did Wanda's hair and makeup for her wedding, This would be the last time I would see Wanda before I dropped out of society and became homeless

A Million Souls

A million souls I long to see
reach heaven through your love for me.
And then when all is said and done
to meet the million souls you won.

I know it's not too much to ask
you know their names from first to last.
With love you wait so patiently
to see the worst of sinners free.

So be my strength Lord and my guide
to search the world both far and wide.
And use my life so they believe
in you eternal life receive

For by your mercy and your grace
I'll one day see you face to face.
With only one thing left to do
return a million souls to you.

Inspired by Danny Velasco... 1 Timothy 1:15-16
By Vince De Maria

On the next few pages there's a letter I wrote to Wanda from rehab, apologizing for disappearing from life and to tell her the good news...

I have been saved!

Dec. 21ˢᵗ '95

Dear Wanda,

Well, I don't even know where to start or what to say first. Theres so much to tell.

First, let me apologize to you and Ward for disappearing the way I did. It was something I had to do. I couldn't keep living the way I was living. I was dying, not really living.

On May 3ʳᵈ I went into a 90 day Rehab in the Catskills. As the time drew nearer to leave there, the fear of returning

2/ to New York to soon gripped me. I knew that although I had been abstinent from drugs for 3 months, the compulsion to use was still with me. I knew if I returned to New York with the emptyness I felt inside, I would use again.

On Aug 3rd I entered a Christian program in Utica, N.Y. Why here? I don't know! I had prayed for guidance and this is where I was led.

On Aug 8th I came forward at an alter call and accepted Jesus as my savior. And the

3/ moment I did everything began
to change for me and change fast.
I started discipleship classes and
began ~~to~~ volunteering all my free
time working with the Pastor here
at the mission. Now, six months
later, I work full time, Sun thru
Thurs, in charge of the house and
its 21 residents. By putting me
in charge of the house Pastor Ric
can devote full time to bringing
the Word to the men on a one
to one basis.
     For the first time in my
life, I feel alive. Everyday I
grow and learn and marvel at
the work The Lord is doing in my
life. Suddenly the meaning of

4/being Born again is alive and real for me.

Oh there's so much to say so much to catch up on. I long to be there with you all ... Wend, Liz, Roberta ..... all of you who tryed so hard to get thru to me, who tryed to wake me up ... who prayed for me. It was you all whose prayers God in his mercy, answered.

I don't really know when or if I'll return to live in N.y. or if I'll return to hairdressing etc. I ~~decided~~ decided to not make any discision the first year. I decided to take it day ~~by~~ day and simply do what needs to be done here.

5/ I do plan on going to see my family after the New Year. I will make time to come by to see you. I look forward to it.

So, until then, just know that all is well, in fact, words, can dearly discribe how good it is.

All my love to all of you.

Danny

P.S. The man who delievered this letter is my friend. Such a good man. I've given him this letter to be hand delievered but put it in an addressed envelope in case circumstances prevented him from

6/ making it to Brooklyn.
I wish you all a wonderful
Christmas and all the joy
and blessings for the New Year.

Saved and Worshiping at The Brooklyn Tabernacle

Prayer Warrior, Wanda Brickner with her Husband Ward and their Baby Abby

LIZ SILVESTRI

PAM SANDERS

Fellow Prayer Warriors and Dear Friends

My Pastor, Jim Cymbala and his wife Carol, Carol is the Choir Director of the
Brooklyn Tabernacal Choir

My Brother David and Sister-in-law Cynthia Thanksgiving 2005

With my nieces Sienna and Bianca Thanksgiving 2005

My dear friends Roger and Mary Skinner who took me in and treated me like family

My extended family, The Brooklyn Tabernacal Choir

Me and The Brooklyn Tabernacal Tenor's

Matt Sherlock, my spiritual son and his first child Arianna

"I'm a Grandfather"

Matt Sherlock, with wife Sarah, Arianna & Braden

Another one of my spiritual sons, Thomas Ortiz and His wife Camille, Thomas works with me in this ministry.

Thomas, Camille and Children: Danny, Kristine and Imani

Praying backstage before speaking at a church in Pennsylvania

Japan

Giving My Testimony at a Church in Japan

Wanda and Me at Christian Global Network TV

Being Interviewed For Christian Global Network TV

Signing Autographs in Japan after a Brooklyn Tabernacle Choir Concert

Me and Wanda in Korea

Writing the manuscript for this book while in-between takes at a photo shoot
Note the tools of my trade on the table.

The Redeemed Years

CHAPTER 12

Early Recovery: Learning to Crawl

As you do not know the path of the wind, or how the
body is formed in a Mother's womb, so you cannot
understand the work of God, the Maker of all things.
ECCLESIASTES 11:5

I don't know when I finally fell asleep, but I drifted off into the deepest and best sleep I had had in years, just repeating over and over. "Jesus... Jesus.... Jesus... Jesus...."

I awoke in the morning and immediately felt the presence of God within me. I knew that what I had experienced was real. I knew that God was with me. I can't express in words what that meant to me. God wasn't going to leave me.

A nurse brought me something to eat, and I was hungry. She commented that I looked better already. Later, a doctor came around and made the same remark.

I started a battery of tests. They took blood and x-rays. I don't remember all they did, but they were taking good care of me. I was diagnosed with Hepatitis A, B, and C. A social worker came in to ask a lot of questions so that Medicaid would pay for everything.

Even though I had planned not to divulge any personal information, I found myself telling her everything. She asked me what my plans were when I was released. I said I didn't know what I would do.

"Would you consider going into a drug rehab if I could arrange it?" she asked.

"Yes, I would consider it. But I don't have any money or insurance," I said.

"That won't be a problem. I'll see what I can do."

The following day, a man came to see me from a rehab called Project Score. It was a 90-day program that took in men who were considered chronic releasers. This was for men whom everyone else had given up on, and who were deemed hopeless by society. He told me that they would pick me up on the day I was released and bring me out to their facility in Liberty, New York. It was a large estate that also housed a two-year program that I could enter when I completed the 90-day program. I agreed to go. I had nowhere else to go, and this was the best offer I had.

Over the years I had been in and out of many rehab facilities, but this time I truly felt that, through the grace of God, I would be able to get clean and stay clean.

After 10 days, I felt better and stronger, and the hospital was ready to release me. I called the number this guy had given me. He told me that their program had an office just two blocks from the hospital, and I should just walk over. They would take it from there. I did exactly as I was told.

When I arrived at the office, there were other guys waiting to be processed and finally it was my turn. I gave them the information they asked for and within a couple of hours, we were all loaded into a van and driven upstate.

We arrived at the Project Score estate and I was surprised at how beautiful the grounds were. There was a stately house with a nice swimming pool. We drove around the house and saw two doublewide trailers that sat behind it.

This was Project Score. The beautiful house was Inward House, the two-year facility. I walked into the trailer with the other guys and had to go through the entrance process. This meant I was taken into a back room and asked to take off all my clothes.

My clothing was put into a large garbage bag and I was examined in places that I hadn't even thought about in years. I guess that addicts hide drugs in some strange places.

It was humiliating, but, then again, who cared at this point? I was at the bottom of the barrel of life and nothing was too degrading any more.

After the exam, I was told to shower. I was given soap, a towel, and some clothes to put on that were a size or two too small for me, and I was super skinny. They said my clothing was being washed and dried, and I would get it back in the morning. These clothes were all I had in the world and I had been wearing them for a long time.

After showering and getting dressed, I was told to sit without saying a word in the living room of the trailer with the other men who had been admitted at the same time as I had.

I sat down, crossed my legs, and was immediately reprimanded, "Sit up straight! Both feet on the floor! Both hands on your lap! Don't ever let me see you cross your legs again!"

We sat in the living room, while the other men in the program went about setting the tables and serving the food. They moved quietly and efficiently.

We were then called in to eat, and after dinner, a couple of men cleaned up. All the men gathered in the living room and sat quietly.

I sat down and automatically crossed my legs. One of the men quickly told me to uncross them. It wasn't allowed.

"Yes, I know. I'm sorry."

Later, I found out that there were many things that weren't allowed. The reason for all these interdictions was that many of the men in this rehab were so out of touch with the real world, with the notion of right and wrong, and so socially inept, that the discipline in this place was intense. I played by all the rules. I wanted to do well. I wanted to get better.

I knew that somehow, somewhere deep inside, God had changed me. I now had hope. It had been birthed in my heart just 10 days earlier in that hospital room. I knew I had a shot and I was taking it.

Spring was in the air, and the job I had been given was to clear an acre of land that had been fenced off for a garden. I had never in my life done anything like this before, so they taught me.

First, I cleared all the rocks, grass, and sticks from the area. After that, I turned all the soil with a shovel. Then, I measured off the different plots for the different vegetables. Next, I dug holes with shallow trenches on either side. I used a stick to measure the distance between the holes for the seeds, and I followed directions for planting from the seed packets.

It took several weeks, but I loved it. I was able to spend hours out in the fresh air digging in the dirt. Having a purpose to each day was a great feeling.

At lunchtime, I had to stop when the bell outside the trailer rang. I came back to the trailer, washed, and changed my clothes. I ate lunch and waited to be dismissed. Then, I put on my work clothes again and returned to the garden.

I planted potatoes, tomatoes, corn, collard greens, lettuce, and zucchini. In the corner of the garden, where all the water seemed to run down and gather, I planted strawberries. I planted snap peas along the fence. I planted daffodils all around the perimeter of the garden. I was told they would keep the rabbits happy, so that they wouldn't burrow under the fence and eat the new crops. I even made a scarecrow and placed it in the middle of the garden. I was very pleased with myself.

I was looking and feeling strong, too. I gained 35 pounds very quickly. I was given lots of other duties in the house as well and managed to keep everything in order. But there was still an empty place inside of me. There was still something missing.

I knew now what this "something" was; I wanted to know Jesus. I really wanted to know Him. I wanted to know what had happened to me. I wanted to know how this could be possible. I wanted to know how calling on His name could bring about such a dramatic change in me.

Often when I was alone in the garden, I really didn't feel that I was by myself. I felt His presence with me, and it gave me such comfort to know that I wasn't alone any more. I would spend hours in the garden talking to Him. I told Him that I wanted to know Him and asked if He would help me to know Him better. I talked to Him about anything and everything.

As my time at the rehab was coming to an end, I had to meet with the counselors to talk about what I planned to do when my time was over. They wanted me to move in to the main house and sign up for another two-year stint. They felt I was not ready to go back into the mainstream world.

After my encounter with God at the hospital, I never had the urge to use drugs again. I was miraculously changed, after I asked Jesus for help on that fateful day. Still, I agreed that I wasn't ready to leave rehab, but I told them that I didn't want to go into their other program in the main house. I told them that I wanted to go into a Christian facility. I asked if they could help me do that.

They tried hard to get me to give up the idea of a Christian rehab, but I held my ground, and they ended up helping me with information. They told me of a Christian facility upstate in Utica, New York. It was five hours north of New York City. I would have to make the arrangements to get there myself. I was given the permission to use the phone, and I made the call. Within a week, I was on a bus headed to the Utica Rescue Mission.

I arrived in Utica and called the facility from the bus station. They sent a van to pick me up. I was then driven to a great old mansion in the town's historic district and was told that I would have to meet with the pastor before being admitted.

After sitting with a man for about an hour of intake information, I finally got in to see the pastor. He asked me a few personal questions and then inquired about my spiritual life and faith.

I told him everything. I told him about my life, and what it had been like. I told him about Wanda always talking to me about Jesus. I told him about my experience in the hospital room that day, and I told him that I wanted to know Jesus. I wanted to know what had happened to me. I needed answers to the many questions I had.

He looked straight into my eyes and smiled. "All the answers you are looking for are in the Word of God. Do you have a Bible?" he asked.

Should I tell him that I sold my only Bible for a pack of cigarettes and two syringes? I decided to just say, "No Sir, I don't."

He reached back to the bookshelf behind him and took a Bible. He handed it over to me and said, "Start reading in the Book of ... "

Before he could say anything, I blurted out, "John!" That was where the money had been placed in the Bible that Wanda gave me several years before. I realized that it had been six years since I first met her that day on a photo shoot, when I mocked her because she sang for the Lord. Yes, it took six very long and painful years for me to get to this point.

The pastor also told me that he was available for a private, one-on-one Bible study, and that he could give me a set appointment for one hour every week. He also mentioned that we had mandatory Chapel Services on Wednesday and Sunday evenings at 7PM. Local churches came to pick up residents every Sunday morning, and the pastor recommended trying several churches in the area to see where God would guide me.

Where would God want me to go? I wondered.

That was the first time I realized that God could lead and guide me in the direction He wanted me to go. It was a wonderful realization. God, the Creator of Heaven and Earth, could direct and orchestrate my life.

Oh my, what had happened to me? Why would God want anything to do with me of all people? I really needed answers to even more questions now.

The young man who had done my intake took me to my new digs, a dorm room with eight sets of bunk beds. He showed me which bed, set of drawers, and closet space would be mine. It was a far cry from my 5,000-square-foot loft in Tribeca, but it was so much better than life in the streets. This would be my new home, and I was very grateful.

I unpacked the few clothes that had been given to me at Project Score and lay down on my bed. I thanked God that He had answered my prayers and led me to a place where I could get to know Him. That was all I wanted right now—to know the Heavenly Father.

I opened my Bible to the Book of John and began to read. I was fascinated. *In the beginning was the Word and the Word was with God, and the Word was God... The word was made flesh and made His dwelling among us and we have seen His glory...* I just couldn't stop reading.

I was like a hungry man who had just sat down at a feast. I couldn't get enough. I read about Repentance, about turning away from my past and toward God.

I read about Salvation, what the cross meant. I believed that somehow all my past had been forgiven.

I even recognized myself in the Bible. *"Therefore, if any man be in Christ, he is a new creation. The old is gone and the new has come."* How excited, how in awe I was. This wonderful God's love blew me away. There was no way we could get to Him, so he came down to us.

I cried all the way through the New Testament, as I realized that it was here all the time and I never knew it existed. No one had ever told me.

And, at last, I read the words Wanda used to say to me, *"Whoever calls on the name of the Lord will be saved."*

I had so many questions, and I was finding the answers to them in the Scriptures. Pastor Rick would help me with the questions to which I couldn't find the answers on my own. When I asked him about purgatory, he told me that there was no such thing.

What, no purgatory? Why did that priest tell me all those years ago that my mother was there still paying for her sins?

"If Jesus paid for all our sins on the cross, what sin is she paying for, Danny?" Pastor Rick asked. "Either Jesus paid for all or he didn't!"

On one hand, I was elated that my mother wasn't in limbo, waiting to be prayed out. On the other hand, I was really angry that I had been told about the purgatory by our parish priest. But now I was confident that mother was in heaven.

What it boils down to is that instead of confronting people with their sins, it's easier to lie, telling them that they will have another chance, the infamous purgatory, to pay the piper. It was easier than telling them about hell. It was a cop-out response and, meanwhile, people's eternal souls lay in the balance.

What a horrible thing to do to people. What a horrible thing to do to a child!

I wondered if the priest had ever read the Bible. If he had, then he intentionally lied to the people. If he hadn't, he shouldn't have been in the position of preaching to people. I would hate to be standing too close to him on the judgment day!

I was also angry about all the prayers I prayed to Mary. My Bible clearly said that Jesus was the *"only mediator between God and man."* Mary might have been *"blessed among women,"* but only

Jesus was seated at the right hand of the Father. Mary, no doubt, is right where I will be one day—standing before the throne of God, worshipping Jesus.

Life in my new home was fun. There was always something going down—fights, stealing, and people going out and never returning. I guess that was to be expected in a facility like this. I managed to find a few men who were really serious about getting their lives together. The five of us knew that God had somehow intervened in our lives, and that we had been given a second chance. We were ready to grab hold of it and run with it.

We began our own Bible study and the pastor was so approving of it, he helped us with study materials. We also began to help him at the chapel services by leading worship and even speaking from the pulpit.

We took on extra jobs in the house and began working each day in the office with Pastor Rick. When it was my turn for the office duty, I would get whatever work needed to be done fast. Then, I would pull up a chair close to the door of the pastor's office, so that I could listen in on whatever Bible study was going on inside.

Alcoholic Anonymous meetings were mandatory, and we had to attend every day. We carried with us a list with dates that we had to have signed and turned in at the end of each month. I got very involved with these meetings. I figured that I had to be there anyway, so I might as well do it all the way.

When elections were held to choose the new meetings facilitator, I was elected. I facilitated the meetings for a long while but eventually got pretty frustrated by it. The thing that bothered me the most was the all-important third step, "I made a decision to turn my life and my will over to God as I understand Him." That statement was too open-ended for me. What did most people understand about God? People in the AA meetings who were trying to be "wise guys" would say that a doorknob or a chair was their "Higher Power."

Funny, I thought, how people could make such stupid comments. But when you tell them that your Higher Power is Jesus Christ, the whole group comes down on you, saying that you are trying to push your beliefs on them.

I decided to step down as group facilitator and told the rehab that I didn't want to go back to the AA meetings. I would continue to find strength and hope in Jesus Christ, and I felt that the AA meetings were a waste of my time. Being a Christian rehab, they were fine with my decision.

I continued to go to different churches in the area, until I finally decided on one church in particular where I felt welcomed and comfortable. I started with "Foundations Classes" that were necessary for membership. Sixteen weeks was a long time, but then again, I had a long time.

I finished the classes and interviewed for membership. The following week I was introduced as a new member. It was the first thing I had ever joined and worked hard to get. It felt good. It felt responsible. That was a feeling about which I didn't know much.

One day, one of the men in the house asked me whether I had started reading the Old Testament yet. I told him that I had heard sermons from the Old Testament, but I was happy just reading and studying the New Testament.

"I just want to know Jesus. I have no interest in the Old Testament," I said.

I know today that this was a pretty dumb answer. But that was how I really felt back then. I didn't know the richness of the Old Testament. Jesus was all that was on my mind at that time.

"If you want a really good picture of Jesus, you should read the Old Testament," he told me. "It's full of prophecies about the coming of Jesus, and there are some great descriptions of Jesus written hundreds and hundreds of years before He was even born. You will love it."

So, I decided to start reading the Old Testament. I read and read, and thought I would lose my mind reading through Numbers. Every once in a while, I would get small glimpses of Jesus, but mostly I was focused on plagues, floods, boils, jackals eating eyeballs, and dead bones jumping out of graves.

Then I got to Isaiah 53. As I began to read, my heart started to beat faster in my chest. This is Jesus! This is Jesus that Isaiah was describing. Jesus! *He grew up before Him like a tender shoot out of dry ground.* He, Jesus, grew up before Him, God the Father, as a tender shoot, gentle, loving and kind—always doing good deeds. Out of dry ground that was Nazareth, *"can any good thing come out of Nazareth?"*

He had no beauty, or majesty to attract us to him, nothing in His appearance that we should desire Him.

Once, I saw Gregory Peck walking on Fifth Avenue with his wife. As he walked by, people stopped and stared with their mouths open. He was the handsomest man I had ever seen. He was huge and majestic. But not Jesus! If one bumped into Him in a market place back then, one might say, "Excuse me", and keep walking. One would have never known that he/she had just bumped into the Son of God in the flesh.

He was despised and rejected by men, a man of sorrows, and familiar with suffering.

Jesus had become flesh and went through every kind of suffering so He could identify with us in every situation that we may face in our lives. That's how He can comfort us in our sufferings. That's why we can look to Him, knowing that He understands what hardships we are going through.

Surely, He took up our infirmities and carried our sorrows, yet we considered Him stricken by God, smitten by Him, and afflicted.

People in the religious community hated him so much that even after they severely beat him and whipped him to the point that he didn't even look human, yanked his beard out with their hands, jammed a crown of thorns hard and deep on his head, and nailed him to a Roman cross, they pointed fingers at him and said He must have deserved to be punished by God.

Isaiah said *Jesus was pierced for our transgressions, He was crushed for our iniquities, the punishment for our peace was upon Him, and by His wounds, we are healed.*

When I read this, it was as if God used this Scripture as a key to suddenly open, unfold, and reveal some great mystery to me. It instantly became clear to me that Jesus had endured his severe beatings, was pierced, and shed his blood, so that I could be forgiven.

Because He was punished, I now found wonderful peace. For the first time in my life, I was comfortable with who I was. For the first time, I had a positive outlook on life.

And by His wounds, each time those whips were struck across his back, my healing became more secure. He had healed my mind, body, and, most of all, my heart. This healing process was just beginning and it would go on and on.

I made a decision that day, that no matter what happened to me from this point, I would never go back to my old life, doing the things that nailed Jesus to that cross. I had received so much more than forgiveness. I had received a second chance. I was going to cling to this chance and never let go.

I decided that while I was still on Medicaid, I should have a complete physical, head to toe. I made an appointment with a local clinic and showed up for a full day of tests. They did every kind of test imaginable. When it came to the blood test, the woman who tried to draw my blood had a very hard time finding a vein. Years of injecting heroin had caused my veins to collapse, and scar tissue further complicated her task.

She must have poked six holes in my arm and moved the needle around inside looking for the vein. Finally, I could see that she was getting very nervous and I just couldn't take it anymore.

"I'm sorry, but I can't let you stick that needle in me again. Give it to me." I said.

I took off the rubber tie that she had put around my arm and tied myself off much higher using my free hand and teeth. I then took the needle and immediately found a deeper vein. Old habits die hard.

I looked up at her and said, "How much blood do you need?" Her lips went white, and I thought she would faint.

"Three vials," she answered.

I drew one, two, three vials, pulled the needle out of my arm, wiped off with an alcohol pad, and put a small Band-Aid on the puncture.

She sat there trying to recover. "Want a job here?" she asked, and we both laughed.

A few days later, we got the results of all the tests back. I was told that my heart and lungs were very healthy. They couldn't even find Hepatitis A anymore. Hepatitis B and C did show up, but both were in remission. The most amazing thing of all was that I was HIV negative.

That's impossible, I thought. I remembered all the times I had shared needles and especially the time I stuck myself with Slim's bloody needle. I asked to have another HIV test, and they told me I could go to the Health Department, but they were confident of their results.

Early the next morning, I went to the Health Department and had another HIV test—negative again. I couldn't believe it. How could this be, I asked? The Health Department told me that sometimes HIV doesn't show up for a while.

Over the next two years, I had about 10 tests for HIV and, still to this day, they have all been negative. I praise God for that. Given my past, it is a true miracle.

Things in our men's residential house were always hopping. Men would come in and men would go out. I began to notice that the only ones who were making it in this program were those who had put their lives and faith in the hands of Jesus. This made me even more determined to tell everyone I could reach about Him.

CHAPTER 13

The Public Speaker: Learning to Walk

However many years a man may live, let him enjoy them all. But
let him remember the days of darkness, for they will be many.
ECCLESIASTES 11:8

Five months after entering the Rescue Mission program, Pastor Rick asked me if I would give my testimony to the Woman's Auxiliary, a group of elderly women and their husbands who funded the program.

I agreed immediately and spoke to them at a meeting. It was the first time I was behind the pulpit giving my testimony. They were a sweet group of about 50 little old ladies and two elderly men.

As I spoke, they wiped the tears from their eyes. After the meeting, one gentleman came over to me and told me that he owned a Christian radio station in that area. He asked me to give my testimony on his program. Again, I agreed.

About a week later, he came by the Residential House and picked me up to take me to the radio station. In the sound room, I was given a headset and the microphone was adjusted to a level in front of my mouth. We did a sound check and when the radio program started, I was introduced and I gave my testimony. It was broadcast live throughout the Mohawk Valley in upstate New York. When I was finished, the telephone lines were open for callers.

The phones rang off the hook. It was an immediate response, and I prayed for people on the air and for the next hour after we had gone off the air. I was very aware of the fact that I had nothing tangible to offer anyone. All I could do was pray and ask God to have mercy on them.

Listening that evening to the program was a Christian journalist who worked as a Features Editor for the local newspaper. The following day he called the program and asked if he could interview me for an article. I agreed.

He wrote a wonderful story that took up the entire front page of the Features Section. This article opened many doors to speak in churches all over the area. I wanted to open a computer lab for the guys in the Rescue Mission program and, once the article appeared in the paper, I was able to raise enough funds to buy several new computers and printers. I had really wanted to do something for the Rescue Mission. They had taken me in when I had nowhere else to go, loved me, and cared for me in many ways. Buying several computers and printers could never compensate for all they did for me, but it was a start.

After six months in the program, I was allowed to have a weekend pass to visit my family. The only family I had was my brother David, his wife, and daughters in Pennsylvania. The last time I saw them was that unforgettable Christmas morning when my brother put me on a bus back to New York City and asked me to never come back again.

The director of the Rescue Mission phoned David, told him about my recovery, and asked if it would be okay if I came to Pennsylvania for a weekend visit. My brother replied that I would be welcome, if I promised not to do any drugs during my visit. The director assured David that I was completely clean and that my life had taken a dramatic change for the better.

The Mission paid for my bus ticket and I took the Greyhound bus. While riding the bus to Pennsylvania, so many thoughts went through my head. *How would it feel to see everybody again?* I wondered. A year had gone by already and I was not the same person I used to be when I left. *What would my family think when they saw me? Would I be tempted to buy and use drugs?* Well, I would find out soon enough.

As it turned out, my brother, sister-in-law, and nieces were as excited to see me as I was to see them. And through the grace of God, our relationship began to grow and flourish in a whole new way. They were truly amazed by the transformation in my life, but when I tried talking to them about the Lord, they weren't interested.

At first, they were very leery about my new-found faith, thinking that it was just a temporary phase. And who could blame them for being distrustful of the "new" me? But with time, they too wanted to know Jesus. After all, if I, of all people, could undergo such a dramatic metamorphosis, there had to be a God in heaven, they thought. Today, they are very involved in their church in Pennsylvania. In fact, my whole family came into a saving knowledge of Jesus Christ. I thank God for that, for He not only touched my life, but the lives of my loved ones as well.

I had also written Wanda a letter telling her all that had happened to me, since I had last seen her. She wrote back, saying that she was overjoyed to hear that I had asked Jesus to come into my heart. It was an answer to her many prayers.

I had not seen Wanda since her wedding day. I remembered doing her hair for her wedding just before I checked out of life.

She then invited me to stay with her and her husband Ward, if and when I did come back to New York. Her place was going to be my first stop when I got my next weekend pass.

That following weekend, I was able to get my pass and another bus ticket to New York. I only made $5 a day working at the Mission, but I was able to buy a Walkman and a couple of Brooklyn Tabernacle CDs. I slipped on my headset, leaned back in the bus seat, and drifted off to sleep listening to the choir.

When I awoke, we were pulling into Penn Station. I picked up my small bag and caught the subway to Wanda's apartment.

It was great seeing Wanda and Ward again. It was also a bit strange because it was the first time I had seen Wanda while I was sober. She had planned a dinner party for that night and had invited several of her friends, the same ones who used to pray for me.

We had a great time. Our conversation was like none I had ever had at a dinner party before. Everyone talked about the Lord and all the wonderful things He had done for them. It was the first time I was able to participate in a conversation. I marveled aloud at all that God had already done in my life.

On Sunday morning, we were getting ready for church. I had bought a suit upstate for $10 at a church clothing sale. The suit was ancient but still in good shape. I wore it like it was a Hugo Boss suit with a vintage edge. *Just keep your head up*, I thought, *and people will think it's a fashion statement.*

We got to Brooklyn Tabernacle, and I sat in the second row that was usually reserved for the choir and their families. The service started, and the praise and worship were amazing. I got lost in the worship. I forgot about everyone around me and lifted my hands as I praised the Lord. It was such a liberating feeling to worship without abandon.

When the choir began to sing a song called "Medley of Change," I recognized it from the CDs I had bought. It talked about a "great change in me." For some reason, I began to cry. I thought about how much I had changed. I hadn't even tried very hard. It was God who was changing me. God was changing me day by day on the inside. I wondered why more people didn't know about this change that was possible through Jesus. I hadn't known either, but Wanda was the first one who had the courage to tell me. At that moment, I knew that I had to tell as many people as possible about what Jesus could do for them simply by sharing with them what He had done for me.

Sometime during the worship service, the pastor, Jim Cymbala, came to the pulpit, stopped the service and said, "You want to hear a great miracle? You thought God parting the Red Sea was a great miracle? Well, Danny Velasco got saved, and he's sitting right there. Stand up, Danny."

I stood up and the church burst into a symphony of praise, clapping their hands and praising God for all that He had done. I didn't know it, but many people in the church had been praying for me for years.

That Sunday was a wonderful day for me. On Monday evening, I went back upstate on the Greyhound bus and signed back into the program before my curfew. I lay in bed that night and went over every minute of the weekend in my head. I realized that I never even thought about drugs the entire weekend. Once again, I was in awe of this life-changing miracle from God.

By the time I completed my year at the Rescue Mission Program, I was offered a job as a counselor. I was torn between staying and returning to New York City.

I began to pray, asking God to give me clear direction on how to proceed. I certainly wanted to do whatever God had planned for me. I didn't want to make any decisions on my own and get myself into a situation that was not God's will for my life.

On my next weekend pass, I called Wanda and Ward and asked them if I could stay with them again.

Wanda answered, "Oh, good! Would it be possible to cut my hair this weekend because on Monday I'm commentator on a fashion show on a daytime talk show for NBC?"

"Sure, that won't be a problem at all," I answered. I was happy to do something tangible for Wanda to thank her for all she had done for me.

That weekend, I cut Wanda's hair and we went to church on Sunday morning. On Monday, Wanda was up and out of the house early. Ward had also already left for work. I was going to have an easy morning and head back upstate after dinner.

Sometime in the late morning, Wanda called. "Hey, Danny," she said. "Today while they were filming this fashion show, the host leaned over to me during a commercial break and asked who cut my hair. She said that she wasn't at all happy with the hairdresser who worked for the show and also did her makeup. I told her that you live mostly upstate, but happen to be in town today. She wants to know if you would come to NBC and cut her hair."

I knew who the show's host was by her name, but I had never met her. She had a very successful talk show once before. I agreed to come into Manhattan and cut her hair that same day.

When I got to NBC, security already had my name. I was given a pass and told how to get to the studio where the show was filmed. I met with the show's host, and she asked me questions about hairstyles and makeup.

I brought some pictures of my work that I had kept through the years, and she seemed to like them. She asked me if I was interested in doing her hair and makeup for the rest of the season. They only filmed on Monday, Tuesday, and Wednesday, two shows a day. I told her that something could be worked out if the money was right. I gave her my old agent's name and number and asked her to tell "her people to call my people." That same day, my agent received the call, and we agreed that I would work on the show three days a week for $2500 per week, plus expenses.

Expenses meant gas to and from upstate each week, and parking at the Rockefeller Center garage. The parking alone was $64 a day plus tip. It wasn't nearly as much as I used to get paid in my heyday, but I was out of circulation for so long. I was just happy to be given an opportunity to work again.

Since I was finished with the program and basically was just staying there to help out and work with the men, I knew that taking a job in New York wouldn't be a problem with the Mission.

I borrowed $1,000 from my agent against future earnings and bought clothes that I could wear to work. After a couple of weeks of working on the show, I purchased a car and rented a house upstate within walking distance of the Mission.

Each week, I drove down to Manhattan and stayed with Wanda and her husband in their spare bedroom. I would arrive on Sunday and go straight to Brooklyn Tabernacle for their 3:30 PM and 6:00 PM services. At that time, they were doing four services every Sunday.

On Monday, I would go to work at NBC and after work on Tuesday, I went to the Brooklyn Tabernacle prayer meeting. After work on Wednesday, I drove back upstate to work at the Rescue Mission on Thursday, Friday, and Saturday. On Friday nights, I would have a Bible study at my house upstate.

One weekend, when I arrived in New York, Wanda said she wanted to talk to me. She broke the news that she and Ward were expecting their first child. I was very happy for them, but my room would be turned into a nursery. That meant that I needed to find my own place.

I told Wanda that I was going out to talk to the real estate agent on the corner. She informed me that the real estate agent only sold houses and did no rentals.

I went anyway.

When I told the agent that I was looking to rent, she laughed and said that she had worked at that agency for 38 years and had never had a rental. However, if I wanted to look for something to buy, she could help me. I replied that I couldn't afford to buy, but I would leave my name and phone number with her just in case. I walked back to Wanda's trying to figure out plan "B."

About two hours later, Wanda's phone rang. It was the real estate agent.

"You're not going to believe this," she said, "but one hour after you left, my phone rang and it was someone whose mother lived in the area. He told me that his mother had passed away and he didn't really want to sell the place. He wants to rent it. I couldn't believe my ears. Do you want to go and see it?"

"No, I don't have to see it. Where is it?" I asked. She gave me the address. Incredibly, it was just a block away from Wanda's house in the neighborhood where I was hoping to live.

"I'll be right over with a check," I told her excitedly. "Do you have the keys?"

"Yes, the owner brought them over. But don't you want to see it first?" she asked.

"No, the Lord gave me this place. I'm sure it's exactly what I need." I said.

Within 30 minutes, I had signed a lease, paid, and had the keys in my hand without even seeing the apartment. You might say it was a leap of faith.

When I finally saw it, I wasn't disappointed. It was exactly what I wanted. It really was a gift from the Lord. Again, I had my own apartment and a great job in New York. I also had my place upstate. I was able to attend church every week for Sunday services and Tuesday night prayer and still minister to the men in the program upstate.

My life was truly blessed. *God works all things for the good of those who love Him and are called according to His purpose.*

Wanda's former roommate, Liz, was involved in the youth ministry at church and for years she had discipled young people. Even though I wasn't one of the young people with whom she worked, I was still, in many ways, a babe in Christ. Liz took me under her wing and I began to grow in God. Mostly, I learned to pray and to really study the Bible at a much deeper level. I knew the answers for any questions I had in life were to be found in the Scriptures.

Several years later, Pastor Cymbala, the senior pastor of the Brooklyn Tabernacle, also felt that the hand of God was on my life, and he invited me to join him in a private mentor/tutoring class he was teaching. He had hand-picked 20 men for these three-to-four-hour, year-long Wednesday night classes. I felt very honored and humbled that I had been asked. I'm sure there are pastors around the world who would pay enormous sums of money for the opportunity to participate in such an outstanding program.

One of the things that I love about my pastor is that he would never accept any money for classes. If he felt that God's hand was on someone's life, he poured himself out helping him/her in any way he could. In Pastor Cymbala's class, we not only learned how to break down the Scriptures and decipher the original meanings in the language in which they had been written, but also how to apply the teachings to our lives and communicate these truths to other people.

Some of us have gone on to become pastors, teachers, and evangelists. Others have become missionaries and heads of ministries. All have come out of this experience with a deep love for Jesus Christ and a passion for the Gospel, the Good News that God so loved the world that He gave His only begotten son to die as a sacrifice for our sins, so that we might have eternal life with Him one day.

Think about that for a minute. We could never be good enough on our own merit to enter heaven and stand on our own righteousness before a Holy God. But when we put our faith in Jesus and entrust our lives to Him, God sees us not in our own righteousness but in the righteousness of Christ Jesus. We become acceptable in God's eyes.

What kind of love is this? It's a kind of love that we, with our finite minds, will never understand. Our love, no matter how intense, could never even scratch the surface of God's redeeming love for us.

How the angels must look down on us and shake their heads in wonder when we reject God's love. Our disregard for God's love must baffle them. No wonder all of heaven rejoices when even just one person makes a decision to accept God's love and commits his or her heart and life into His hands.

At Christmastime that same year, I was invited to my pastor's home for dinner. Afterwards, someone pulled out a small laptop keyboard and began to play Christmas carols, and we all sat around singing. It was a sweet time of fellowship that meant so much to me.

My mind flashed back to one Christmas several years before, when I was in an apartment of a woman who I had met on the streets. I had been planning to go to my brother David's house in Pennsylvania and had even bought gifts for my two nieces. But on Christmas Eve, I was broke and sick from lack of drugs. I took the gifts that I had bought for my family out to the streets and sold them. I then used the money to buy drugs.

I never made it to Pennsylvania. It snowed heavily that year and I walked in knee-high snow on Christmas Eve, trying to sell the gifts, and then looking for someone from whom to buy drugs. All the rest of that night I sat staring out of the window on the 33rd floor, looking out at the falling snow and watching couples walking around down below, feeling sorry for myself. The memory of that Christmas made this time spent with friends at Pastor and Carol Cymbala's house a lot more special to me—much more special than anyone knew.

The following Sunday, in church, an announcement was made that applications for choir auditions were being given out in the lobby after the service. I had always thought it would be fun to sing in the choir. I loved worshipping the Lord and I loved singing, but never really thought I had a good enough voice to be in the world-famous Brooklyn Tabernacle Choir. Even though I never really thought that singing was one of my "gifts," I stood in line, took a choir application, and filled it out. Right before turning it in, I thought more about it deciding that I probably wasn't talented enough for the choir anyway, turned around, and walked away, still holding the application in my hand.

I headed down a hallway that went from the sanctuary to the main offices of the church and bumped into one of the choir leaders, Kevin Lewis.

"You were supposed to turn that application in at the table you got it from," he said.

"I know, but I decided not to turn it in. I don't think I sing well enough to be in the choir." I answered.

"Give me that!" Kevin said, as he took the application out of my hand.

A couple of days later, I received the date for the audition in the mail. It would be held on a Wednesday night, when I had classes scheduled with Pastor Cymbala.

Oh well, I thought. *Maybe this is God's way of telling me that he would rather have me speaking to audiences than singing in the choir.* I never showed up for the audition.

The following Sunday, I got a message from the Pastor's wife, Carol, saying that she wanted to talk to me between the services. She apparently had "a bone to pick with me." My mind went into overdrive trying to figure out what I had done. Had I said something offensive? I felt like a little kid being called into the principal's office for a scolding.

After the service, I went into the staff lunch area looking for Carol.

"You didn't show up for my audition on Wednesday night," she said.

"I know, but I had my class with the Pastor that night," I explained. "Anyway, I don't think I can make it through the audition process. I don't have a great voice. I mean, I can hold a tune, but I'm not good enough to sing in the Brooklyn Tabernacle Choir."

"You already had an audition with me. You sat next to me in my home and sang Christmas carols. Remember? And, Danny, although there are some pretty amazing voices in the choir, I want people who love to worship Jesus. I've watched you worshipping the Lord. You have a lot to be grateful for and it shows when you worship. I think you should be in the choir."

"Well, let me think about it." I said.

"Okay, think about it. But come to the choir practice on Friday night."

I showed up that Friday and I've been in the choir ever since. I find it amazing and truly miraculous that I now sing in the same choir that I had once mocked, and then came to hear perform at Radio Music City Hall, when I lived in the streets. I was moved by it then, but who could have predicted that one day I too would be singing in this choir? Only the Lord could have known and made this happen.

I love singing to the Lord. It's a wonderful anointing that God sends when the choir begins to sing. It's kind of a joke among the choir members that we never really know what we are going to sing until we actually hear the first few notes of the music. Every Friday we learn two songs and often sing them on Sunday. Other times, we get up in front of the congregation and end up singing something completely different.

Carol always leads the choir in a way that is sensitive and responsive to the Holy Spirit of God, and follows the Spirit's promptings. Sometimes we perform a newly learned song; at other times we rediscover something we haven't sang in months.

I believe that God honors Carol's obedience and therefore anoints the choir in a very special way. People are touched by God's anointing and lives are changed because the music opens their hearts to Him. *God dwells in the praises of His people.*

The Lord has allowed the choir to win six Grammy awards as of this writing, but the real trophies are the many hearts that are won for the Lord Jesus Christ not only in our church but also around the world.

Being in the choir has taught me discipline and has taught me so much about the sense of family and community. It is one of the most wonderful things about my new life. In the choir, we sing as one, we worship as one, and we minister as one. We love and encourage each other, going out of our way to work together in harmony and peace.

All this carries over into all the other parts of my life. People see something different in us—they see Jesus.

Let's face it—the only Jesus many people will ever see is in the face of a Christian. If Christians are showing any other face or living any other lifestyle, they dishonor not just themselves, but they dishonor the Lord Jesus too. They also are missing out on the greatest privilege any human being could ever have—representing the Lord Jesus to the world. After all, the Bible says that we are *ambassadors for God, as if God is crying out through us to be reconciled to Him.*

One night, I was at a dinner party at a choir member's home, and I struck a conversation with a couple from another church. The husband asked me how I was saved, and I related my story to him. When I finished, he asked if he could tell his pastor about me. Maybe he would invite me to be a guest speaker in his church.

I agreed.

A few days later, I got a call from a church in Manhattan. The secretary told me that the pastor would like to meet with me about possibly sharing my testimony with his congregation. We made an appointment for the following Wednesday evening after work. I asked for the name and address of the church.

"East Side Tabernacle," she said and gave me the address.

I couldn't believe it. It was the same church where Liz had brought the youth choir years before, where the pastor had asked to seat me up front, but I had run out. I wondered whether it was just a coincidence or God's plan.

On Wednesday, as I sat in the church's reception area waiting to see the pastor, I wondered whether he would remember that night so long ago. When he finally came out of his office, he approached me with his hand extended and suddenly stopped.

"I know you!" he cried out. "You're that homeless man who was standing at the back of the church and then ran out of here. Oh! Praise God! I have been praying for you for years. Oh! Praise God! Praise the Lord! Look what the Lord has done!" He began to cry, and so did I.

We went into his office and talked for a long time. He had asked me to tell the story of that day so long ago, when I had been in the church and ran out.

A couple of Sundays later, I was standing behind the pulpit speaking to the congregation. As I talked, I looked up at the balcony where I had shot dope so many times before when this building was a nightclub. Once again, I was in awe of God.

He takes what was meant for evil and turns it for the good. He makes all things beautiful in His time. Even this building that was once dedicated to evil, now housed the people of God.

After about five years of going back and forth between Utica and New York City, I decided to move back home full time. The years of serving the Lord at the Utica Rescue Mission were great in so many respects, but now my work was in New York, where my agent was again able to book me on photo shoots. And I was more and more involved in the ministry at the Brooklyn Tabernacle.

So, I went looking for a house somewhere on Long Island. I wanted a large house with as many bedrooms as possible, and I wanted it on the ocean.

Having grown up in Tampa, on Florida's Gulf of Mexico coast, I had always wanted to live at the beach. The extra bedrooms would not stand empty because I had decided to take in several of the men I had been counseling upstate. I knew that they were good men and loved the Lord, but had never been given a chance to be reintegrated into the mainstream life. I wanted them to have that second chance.

I found exactly what I was looking for on the Island's south shore. I bid goodbye to the Rescue Mission program and moved back home to New York full time.

During another Christmas holiday season, I went to Wanda and Ward's home for dinner. By then, they had a beautiful little boy named Smith. Wanda said that she had something she wanted to show me when we finished eating.

We had a lovely meal and then went into the living room. Wanda went to the bookshelf and took out an old Bible of hers.

"I was unpacking a box of old books and ran across it," she said. "So, I began to flip through and read the notes I had made while listening to different sermons and reminiscing. I ran across this piece of paper. I want to give it to you."

It was a prayer list.

She told me that she wrote down her prayer requests, and as God answered each prayer, she would draw a line through it. When the list was full, she made a new one, and carried over any unanswered prayers to it.

I looked at the sheet of paper she handed me. All of the prayer requests had lines drawn through them, except one. It said, "OH GOD! Please save Danny. We need a miracle!"

Then I looked at the date at the top of the list. It was six years after she had first met me at the photo shoot. It had been carried over to new lists, many, many times.

I did some quick math and calculated that she had prayed this prayer over 2,000 times. Besides her own prayers, she had so many other people praying for me at the church. I can't even imagine how many prayers came before the throne of God for me. No wonder He moved into my life!

Jesus told a parable about a persistent widow who kept coming to a judge with her plea for justice against her adversary. This judge neither feared God nor cared for men, so he kept refusing the widow's pleas. But finally he said to himself, "Even though I don't fear God or care about men, because this widow keeps bothering me, I will see that she gets justice, so that she won't eventually wear me out."

Jesus told us that if this judge, who didn't care about God or men, answered the widow's persistent pleas, how much more would our Father, who loves us, give us if we were as persistent in our pleas. That's also why we are told to *knock and keep on knocking, and the door would be opened to us. To ask, and keep on asking and we would receive.*

I told Wanda she could draw a line through that prayer request. God answered that prayer and because He did, I had been reborn.

What a faithful God! Who else has ever given us permission to *"come boldly before the throne of grace where we can find mercy in our times of trouble?"* That is where we make our requests known to God.

God sometimes even grants us our heart's desires, even if we don't ask.

I was once speaking at a church in Pennsylvania, and my brother, sister-in-law, and two nieces, Bianca and Sienna, were sitting in the front row. At the end of the sermon, I was trying to convey to the congregation how vital Jesus was in my life.

"Everything in my life is happening only because of Jesus," I said. "If there is anything that you like about me, it's because of Jesus. You wouldn't have wanted to know me apart from Jesus. Everything I have in my life today is only because of Jesus. Even my very breath today is from Jesus. You see my family sitting here in the first row, and they are only in my life today because of Jesus."

Then, I heard these words come out of my mouth, "You see, Jesus is my everything."

Suddenly, I flashed back to that day in the car with Damaris, when I mocked her for saying the very same words. I made a silent note to myself that the next time I saw Damaris, I had to tell her and apologize.

After the sermon, I said goodbye to my family and got into my car to drive back to Brooklyn. I was contemplating trying to get back to make the 3:30 service at Brooklyn Tabernacle.

When I turned on my phone in the car, I noticed that there were several messages from the church. I called, and the secretary, Suzanne Greaves, told me that she had been trying to get me all morning. Pastor Cymbala wanted me to speak at the 3:30 service. No need to wonder now if I should try to get back in time.

I told her that I was in Pennsylvania and had just finished speaking at a church there. I had plenty of time to get back, so I would be there for the service.

Driving back, I asked God what I should speak about and felt that He wanted me to address the same topic I had spoken on that morning—2 Corinthians 5:20-21, about being an *Ambassador for God*. I went over the message again in my head. I wanted to mentally review it, so that I could communicate the message even better.

As I was driving back to New York on I-78, I prayed, "God, help me today at Brooklyn Tabernacle. The people all know me and I want to bless them."

I began to think of God's goodness and talked to Him as if He were in the car with me.

"Lord," I said, "Why are you so good to me? Why have you chosen to put me up in front of people to be a spokesman for you? After the life I have led, why would you want anything to do with me?"

All of a sudden, a Scripture verse came to my mind. It was something that I hadn't thought of or even read in years. It was Moses asking God almost the same question that I was now asking—Lord, why have you chosen *me*? Moses says to God, "I can't even speak so well. Why don't you use Aaron, my brother? He is the one who speaks well." (Paraphrasing a bit.)

"Moses, for this I have raised you up," God answers. *"That I may fill you with power, that my name might be glorified in all the world."*

God was answering me through this Scripture, which is one of the ways He speaks to us. Now I knew I had God's attention and wanted to keep the "communication lines" open. I continued to question God; I wanted to keep hearing from Him.

"But Moses was basically a good guy," I said. "He killed a man once, but when God spoke those words to him, 40 years had gone by. And for those 40 years, he lived a decent, well-adjusted life. Me, I was living like an animal just a few years ago and I wasn't such a nice guy. I was the worst kind of low life. So, Lord, why me?"

Another Scripture suddenly jumped into my head. This time it was the apostle Paul writing to Timothy:

"This is a true and faithful saying. That Jesus Christ came into the world to save sinners of whom I am chief. But for that reason I was shown mercy so that in me, the worst of sinners, Christ Jesus might display His unlimited patience as an example for those who would believe on Him and receive eternal life."

I was almost moved to tears. As I was sitting in my car, I really felt that I was conversing with God. He was giving me the answers I needed to hear.

I arrived at the Brooklyn Tabernacle just as the 3:30 service started. I was too late to sit up in the choir risers, so I slipped into a section reserved for choir members' families.

When Pastor Cymbala called me up to speak, I stepped up to the pulpit and looked out at the congregation. There, sitting in the fifth row were Damaris and her husband Rod.

As I spoke, I wove in the part about Jesus being "my everything," and I publicly apologized to Damaris. I was sure that God had given me this opportunity.

I love the way God orchestrates even the little things in our lives. He's concerned with the details. He wants to make our lives complete and whole. He gives us the opportunities to make our past wrongs right, so that we can be at peace with ourselves.

He is truly the *Prince of Peace.*

God continues to bless me even though I have failed Him in the past. So many times I have come to Him asking for forgiveness.

The Bible says that if we *"confess our sin, He is just and faithful to forgive our sin and cleanse us from all unrighteousness."*

I have proven this over and over. I'm not proud of my sins, but I can surely boast that *His mercies are new each and every morning.* He is certainly the God of second chances, and even third and fourth chances. As a matter of fact, He is the God of as many chances as we need to become the kind of people He wants us to be.

Each day I know that I need Him more and more. What would I do, and where would I be without Him? I doubt that I would be alive today, if it were not for His divine intervention. And even if I were still alive, I would be hopelessly lost in the darkness. But Jesus took me by the hand and led me into His glorious light. He said, *"I am the Light of the world. Follow me and you won't stumble in the darkness."*

With Jesus by my side, I am strong. Right in the places where I am the weakest is right where His strength is made perfect. Jesus has not only given me the ability to step out of the darkness, but also to walk away and never look back.

When He walked on earth, teaching and revealing His wisdom, He always kicked things up a notch. For instance, the Law of Moses said— Do not kill. Jesus said, "Anyone who hates his brother (another human being) has committed murder in his heart and therefore is a murderer."

The Law said, "Do not commit adultery."

Jesus said, "If anyone looks at another lustfully, he has committed adultery in his heart."

The Law said, "Love your neighbor as yourself."

Jesus said, "Love one another, as I have loved you."

His blessings also go so much further.

When I called on the name of the Lord, I just wanted to get out of a jam. But Jesus said, "Not only will I get you out of a jam, but I'll give you a new life as well. I will cleanse your consciousness. No more shame, no more guilt."

You would think that this would be enough, but not for this God, who goes even further in His generosity toward us. *"Then I will save your whole family and they will worship me from generation to generation."*

And if that wasn't enough, *"Then I will stand you up before the whole world, so that others will know that there is still a God in heaven."*

It is as if we become trophies of His grace, His mercies, His unlimited power, and His love. God actually looks for opportunities to bless us.

And that is when the Scripture really comes alive for me. *"He is able to do exceedingly, abundantly above all we could ask or think, according to the spirit that works in us."*

The spirit that works in us as Christians is the same spirit that raised Jesus from the dead. Even as I write about my past here in these pages, it's almost as if I'm describing a movie I once saw. I remember all the details and all the scenes, but I am emotionally unattached to the person I once was. It's because Jesus removes us from our sin as far as the east is from the west.

Today, I am someone brand new, renewed by the Spirit of the living God—a wonderful, miraculous God. I don't even have the words to accurately describe His greatness.

CHAPTER 14

Giving It Away: Learning to Run

Fear God and keep His commandments, for this is the whole duty of man.
For God will bring every deed into judgment, including
every hidden thing whether it is good or evil.
ECCLESIASTES 12:13–14

Over the years that have passed since that horrible, and yet very wonderful day in a hospital room in the Bronx, God has given me the privilege to speak in countless churches across America and the world.

To this day, I still often wonder how this great God could love someone like me. I only know that He loves me, but not why or how. My only explanation is, because He is God, and *God is Love.*

This love of His has filled the innermost places in my soul—the places were emptiness used to prevail. I don't worry anymore because He has promised to never leave me. I sense His presence every day as clearly as I did that first night in the hospital, and as clearly as I have each day since then.

Today, I am learning to rely on the Holy Spirit more and more. Through my Pastor's insights into the Word of God, as well as his sensitive and practical way of communicating, I have come to understand because of what Jesus did for me on the cross, my past has been forgiven. I have also learned that every single thing that I have ever said, done, or thought that was unacceptable in the eyes of God, has been not only forgiven, but also forgotten by Him.

Now I am at peace with God and I have the peace OF God. It's a peace that Jesus left with us and nobody in the world can take from us. Jesus has risen from the dead and has ascended back to heaven where He is seated at the right hand of the Father making intercessions for us.

But what about the future?

That's where the Holy Spirit enters the picture. When Jesus was about to return to heaven, He said that He wouldn't leave us as orphans. He promised that when He returned to the Father, He would ask the Father to give us another Counselor to be with us forever. Jesus called Him the Spirit of Truth. Jesus said the Holy Spirit would teach us all things. He is the one who convicts the world of its sins. The Holy Spirit is the one who empowers us as Christians and gives us the ability to overcome the obstacles the world throws our way. He is also the one who helps us love even the most unlovable among us. The Holy Spirit is God's only agent on earth at this time. He has come not only to help us and to strengthen us but also to teach and comfort us. Coming to rely on the Holy Spirit is crucial in my life today, and that reliance on Him should also be crucial to all the Christians around the world.

For most of my life, I have lived with a great empty place deep inside my soul. I tried to fill it with everything under the sun—phony confidence, work, sex, money, alcohol, and drugs. Nothing I ever tried gave me more than a temporary pleasure. But since Jesus has filled that empty place with His love, I don't ache any more.

I realize now that there is a place inside all of us that is reserved only for Him. It is as if it were built right into our DNA. We will never feel whole and complete until Jesus fills that empty place inside of us. Instead of growing tired of or used to it, this just gets sweeter and sweeter as the years go by.

The Bible says *"God delights in us. He quiets us with His love and rejoices over us with singing."*

Think about this for a moment. As much as we might love singing to Him, he delights in us so much that He begins to sing over us! Wouldn't you love to hear that beautiful sound of God singing over us? Sometimes, when I am singing with the choir, I try to listen to Him singing. Someday I will hear this sound in person. All I know is I can't wait for that day to come.

The apostle John said that the sound of billions of people singing in Heaven was like the sound of oceans upon oceans. I wonder if all of heaven goes silent when God begins to sing. Is everyone there totally captivated by the sound of God singing?

Looking back over my life, I can see how God's hand of protection has always been there. Even when I rejected him as a young child and continued to run from Him as an adult, He never gave up on me.

He could have said, "Ah, forget this guy! You want to do it alone, fine, but don't come to me later crying about this and that."

He had every reason in the world to give up on me, but He didn't. Patiently, He waited and continued to reach out to me. Even though I have failed him so many times, He still says, "I love you. You are mine." Even when my faith has been shaken and I doubted Him, His love was poured out on me.

His supernatural ability to change and transform a life still puts me in awe of Him. The richness of His mercy continues to amaze me. He won't throw us away or forget about us. He continues to bless us and to look for every opportunity to show us how much He cares for us. It is as if He longs to bless us.

But, if you really want to know what God is like, just look at Jesus.

If you want to know what God's character is like, just look at Jesus.

If you want to know what God's love and compassion are like, just look at Jesus.

Jesus is the visible image of the invisible God.

Although I no longer have—nor do I yearn for—the riches and the lifestyle I once had, these past few years have been the best of my life. I wouldn't trade them for all the money in the world.

As I write this, 13 years have passed since that day in the hospital where I first met Jesus. This tells me that God cannot only pick us up, clean us up, turn our lives around, and set our feet on solid rock, which is Jesus Christ, but He can keep us in His care forever.

Recently, I started a ministry out of Brooklyn Tabernacle called Celebrate Recovery. It is a ministry that not only makes referrals to drug and alcohol rehabs for those coming in to the church and wanting a new life, but also for those coming out of rehabs and still struggling with addiction issues. Celebrate Recovery is a place where these individuals can come to and immediately feel welcomed and loved. We provide counseling and discipleship for them. We also have meetings where they can talk freely and confidentially about anything they want. They can get feedback from someone else in the group who went through the same experience or just have someone to whom to talk.

We put them together with men and women who will befriend and encourage them. It's as easy as "Hey, come sit here, I've saved you a seat next to me." Or "Let's go out and eat together after the service today."

I have found that just showing these folks that you care about them, that you like them, and that you enjoy their company is worth its weight in gold. We need each other. We all want to feel loved and accepted. We all long for fellowship and being part of a loving family who accepts us. That is what makes us all human.

This kind of outreach made all the difference in the world to me. Didn't Jesus say, *"Love one another as I have loved you?"* How is this possible? How can we love others the way Jesus loved us?

Well, if we are Christians, then we already have all it takes to love even the most unlovable among us. Galatians 5 names the fruits of the Spirit and the first one is love.

And, if we are Christians, hasn't the Spirit been deposited in our hearts at the moment of Salvation?

As I counsel these young men today, I see when God begins to renew their minds.

I watch the changes begin and I see how love replaces anger and hate.

I see how joy replaces sadness.

I see how boldness and strength replace weakness.

I see hope replace hopelessness.

I see broken hearts mend and made whole.

I see shattered dreams be replaced with new dreams.

I see some of the toughest thugs with tears in their eyes telling me how God has opened their hearts and made their hearts sensitive and tender.

I watch guys who grew up with abusive dads or no dads become great dads.

I see men who came from broken homes or abusive homes become great husbands.

I watch the proud become humble.

I see how resentments melt away as forgiveness replaces them.

I see how minds and hearts in turmoil are replaced with the peace that passes all understanding.

I see that where sin abounded, now there is grace.

They are made alive in Christ, and Scripture comes alive before my very eyes.

Thomas Ortiz is an example. He started doing heroin at age 14. His father was an addict and ran the streets in the Bronx. One day, Thomas came home from school to his mother's apartment in the housing projects to find all their belongings out in the street. His mother was unable to pay the rent and the city had evicted her. His Mother, baby brother, and Thomas went from one welfare hotel to another, and finally ended up sleeping on the rooftops of buildings in the neighborhood.

By the age of 16, Thomas was a full-blown heroin addict, selling drugs to support his habit. He was too addicted to spend any of the money he earned to help feed his mother and younger brother. He even contemplated suicide, feeling that he was unable to go on living. Life was just too hard for this young boy.

One day, sitting on a curb and wondering how to kill himself, another drug dealer said to him, "You need Jesus. He's the only one who can help you."

Can you believe that? God used a drug dealer to reach out to Thomas.

At 16, Thomas went into Brooklyn Teen Challenge, a drug rehab center for teens. When he came out, his witness to his mother was so intense that she too turned her life over to the care of Jesus.

But Thomas still had so much anger and resentment in his heart towards his father for abandoning the family that he relapsed and went back to drugs to numb the pain.

One day, God impressed on Thomas that the only way for him to get better was to forgive his father. Thomas got his chance to heed

God's guidance. His aunt was dying in a hospital, and his father didn't show up to see her before she died. When his father finally did show up, Thomas saw him coming from an upstairs window.

Thomas was ready to open the door and seriously hurt his father. All the anger and pain had built to a point of exploding. But when he did open the door, God's love overwhelmed Thomas. He embraced his father, told him he loved him, and forgave him. It was the first time in his life he had ever told his father he loved him.

Years have gone by, and now Thomas is like a son to me. He lived with me until the day he married his beautiful wife, Camille, and now he is the father of two children. One child belonged to his wife when he married her, and the second one is their child together. He's a great husband and a great dad, who works with me in this ministry. He still takes care of his mother and still ministers to his dad.

There is also Matthew Sherlock. When I first met him, he was in big trouble with the law. He had beat up a drug dealer with a baseball bat. Because the offense was drug related, he was mandated to a drug rehab by the courts. There he had a fight with a counselor and ended up beating him too. When the police arrived, Matt also took a swing at the cops. That's when he went to jail. The Rescue Mission was able to get custody when they heard about the boy. He was still a teenager at that time.

I was called into the office to meet Matt and when I extended my hand to introduce myself, he looked at my hand and turned his face away. I sat down and tried to talk to him. He just looked at me blankly and wouldn't answer. He had completely shut down emotionally. I was asked by the program's director to take Matt to the clinic for a complete physical.

Once we were in my car, I realized that I had forgotten to bring a Release of Confidentiality paper that had to be filled out. My car was already running and I was torn between taking my keys inside with me or leaving the car running, while I quickly went into the building to get the paperwork. I didn't want to come out and find Matt and my car gone.

I decided to show him right from the beginning that I trusted him, so I left the car running.

When I came back out of the building, I was relieved to see the car still there, but I could hear the filthy music blasting from the car radio. He had changed the radio station and turned up the volume all the way. It was deafening.

I got into the car. I reached to turn down the volume and was about to say to him, "Listen, you little punk … " but before all the words came out of my mouth, the Holy Spirit brought such conviction. It was as if He said to me, "I died for him."

I was so shaken by the whole experience that when I finally got Matt into the clinic, I said to him, "I'll be in the car right out front, waiting for you."

I went back to my car and began to cry. I wasn't crying for Matt. I was crying for my lack of compassion, my lack of love, and my inability to minister to this kid.

I began to pray, "God help me. If you want me to continue to minister to this young man, you have to put love in my heart for him, because everything about him rubs me like sandpaper."

At that precise moment, God began to flood my heart with so much love for this boy that I thought I would burst. I saw him as a young child who had been very hurt somewhere along the way.

Over the next couple of years, I ministered to Matt, but he seemed to get worse and not better. He finally ended up in jail again for unrelated charges. Every other week, I would visit him and spend time with him. He called me almost every night and I would always pray with him over the phone.

When he was released one year later, I was there to pick him up and drive him back to New York City. The following day, we met with my pastor and finally decided that Matt needed to go into the Teen Challenge program. I told him that if he could complete one year in Teen Challenge, he could come and live with me.

During that time, I spent every Tuesday night at a prayer meeting sitting with Matt at the church where Teen Challenge held their meetings. When the year was over, I was asked to introduce him at his graduation and present him with his certificate of completion. One of my pastors spoke at his graduation.

I was feeling uneasy because I had promised Matt that he could come live with me if he would make it through all the way. But I didn't really feel that the Lord had signed off on this move.

After the graduation ceremony I took Matt aside and told him that he would have to stay there a little longer.

"How much longer?" he asked.

"I don't know," I answered. "Until I feel that it's okay with God."

He seemed to take this better than I thought he would.

The spring went by and sometime in early summer, he called and told me that Teen Challenge was having a weekend outreach to the community. There would be a "hoops throwing" contest for the young people, games for all and, of course, the tent revival meetings. He asked me if I would come. His job at this event would be to take the little kids for go-cart rides.

I showed up on Saturday afternoon and, as I walked across the field where all the activities were taking place, I spotted Matt right away. He was standing just at the edge of the revival tent with his back to me and his arms up in the air. It looked as if he was holding on to the ropes that held the large tent down.

But as I came up behind him, I realized that he wasn't holding on to any ropes. His arms were raised in worship, and he was praying and praising God out loud. I was so moved that I lifted my hands to heaven as well, and began to thank God for what I could see He had done in Matt's life.

When Matt heard my voice behind him, he turned, embraced me, and said, "Jesus loves me. He really loves me and He has set me free!"

We hugged for what seemed like a long time and all I could think to say was, "You can come home now, Matt."

Over that summer, Matt worked at the Brooklyn Tabernacle. The little kids at the church loved him. Little boys would climb all over him. Matt would pretend they were stronger than he was. Little girls would also run to him to show off their new dresses. When he would say, "You look beautiful!" they blushed and twirled around for him.

I couldn't help but think to myself, "Look what God can do! This was the same guy who had beaten someone with a baseball bat. Now he's so gentle that the kids adore him."

Matt decided that summer that he wanted to go to Bible College. We were able to get him enrolled at Zion Bible and in September of that year, I drove my spiritual son to Rhode Island.

During the school year, he called almost every day.

One day, he asked me if I would drive out to Rhode Island and take him out to dinner. He had met a young woman and wanted me to meet her.

I drove out a couple of weekends later and met a very sweet girl named Sarah, who was so shy she could hardly speak to me. She was adorable.

A year later, Matt proposed to Sarah and today they are married and have the most beautiful baby girl, Arianna, who can't stop giving kisses. Matt is a great husband and a great dad.

Only the true and living God can do these things. I could tell you story after story of God's miraculous, life-transforming power.

No one is so far-gone that God's arms of mercy can't reach him.

No one has done anything that His love can't forgive.

Nothing can ever separate us from the Love of God that is in Christ Jesus.

We become one with Christ and one in Christ.

We become the children of God.

We become members of the family of God.

We become ambassadors for God.

Together we are the body of Christ with Him as the head.

We stop stumbling in the darkness, because He is the light of the world.

We long to be Holy because He is Holy.

His love compels us to follow and want to be pleasing to Him.

Recently I have had the opportunity to go to Korea and Japan with the Brooklyn Tabernacle Singers and speak through interpreters to large auditoriums of people. The Koreans and Japanese are gentle and kind people, and they treated us like honored guests. The food there is very different and very delicious. But in order to find out if I liked it or not, I had to taste it. Otherwise I would have never known how wonderful it was.

Well, the Bible says that we should, *"taste and see that the Lord is good."*

How else will we know what He can do, if we don't give Him a chance?

How can we know His forgiveness, if we have never asked to be forgiven?

How can we reject His love, if we have never experienced it?

Salvation can be experienced so easily that a child can do it. Yet, it is so profound that the greatest minds in the world cannot explain it.

And it all begins with a simple prayer.

A prayer prayed from a sincere heart.

This prayer simply asks Jesus to come into your heart and be the Lord of your life.

This prayer says that you will put your trust in Him.

This prayer says you are willing to turn your back on those things that aren't pleasing to Him.

It is as simple as this: *"Whoever calls on the name of the Lord will be saved."*

So, I want to encourage you. Jesus is as close as the mention, even the mere whisper of His name.

The Bible says that *His eyes go to and fro on the earth just searching for a heart that is turned to Him.*

Won't you open your heart to Him today?

Won't you ask Him to change you?

We all have hurts that are so deep that nothing or no one can reach them or change them, except Jesus.

We all have broken promises, broken dreams, and broken pieces in our hearts.

God's Word has new promises for you. Jesus will give you new dreams and mend the broken pieces in your heart.

He does it by changing you on the inside.

You won't even have to try, you just have to trust.

I know that if He could do it for me, He can do it for anyone.

One of the things God has always given me is passion.

When I was young, I dreamed about my future with a passion.

As I got older, I pursued my life with a passion.

Even as a drug addict, I pursued drugs with a passion.

Now, I pursue Jesus with a passion. I read His word with a passion. I pray with passion.

One day, I hope to stand before Him and see Him face to face. I pray that on that day, He will look at me with passion and say, *"Well done, my good and faithful servant. Well done."*

And who knows, perhaps my mother will be standing somewhere in the throngs of people around the throne, and maybe she also will say, "Well done!"

CHAPTER 15

Final Thoughts

The world has nothing to offer me now. I have had it all, and I have had nothing at all. So what have I learned? I have learned that the only thing worth having is a relationship with Jesus.

Even though God has restored my family to me and has allowed me to go back to the business I love as a full time career, I view that business much differently now. Besides doing what I am gifted to do, the fashion business has become a wonderful mission field. It is full of people leading empty and shallow lives, and they need to hear about the love of Jesus Christ. I have spoken at events where two full rows have been reserved for guests that I have invited from the industry.

Several times I have been the guest speaker at a wonderful ministry called Models for Christ/PARADOX. This is actually a ministry in New York that witnesses the love of Christ to models, photographers, hairdressers, makeup artists, wardrobe stylists, art directors, and basically anyone connected to the fashion business. Wanda was part of Models for Christ all those years ago when she had been witnessing to me.

A couple named Jeff and Laura Calenberg, both models, both Christians who love the Lord, started MFC. They have been faithful for over 20 years to bringing the Gospel to many people in this dark jungle that we call the Fashion Industry. Many of them may have never heard the Gospel, so it has been a real joy to share my life story at several Models for Christ outreaches.

As I spoke at these events, I looked out to a room packed with young people who, like I did so many years ago, have come to New York to find fame and fortune. I trust that God will use me in some way to help them avoid the valley of despair that I walked through to find Jesus.

When we stand before God, we bring nothing of this world with us. We can only stand before God with our sin or without our sin.

Jesus came to earth to free us from our sin because sin, the Bible says, will never enter heaven. If we stand before God with our sins, entrance into heaven will be denied to us. We will be cast away from heaven and away from the presence of God for all eternity. There is no sin so grave that God cannot forgive except maybe for one—rejection of God's offer to be forgiven and to spend eternity with him.

When that day comes for us to stand before Him, it will be too late to change your mind.

Won't you take His offer today? Making a decision to ask Jesus to forgive you and to put your trust in Him will be the single most important decision you will ever make in your earthly life.

When Jesus was preparing to return to heaven, He said, "I go to prepare a place for you."

But He didn't go to prepare a place for everybody. You see, heaven is a prepared place for prepared people.

Are you prepared?

There is only one thing you have to do to be prepared for heaven that is putting your faith and your life in the hands of Jesus.

What will you do with eternity?

What will you do with Jesus?

We are not guaranteed tomorrow.

We need to make a decision today.

I pray that you will make the right one.

Benediction:

May God richly bless you, and may the God of peace who passes all understanding reign in your hearts now and forever more.

Thank you for picking up this book. If you know anyone who might be blessed or inspired by it, please pass it along.

Epilogue

On October 4, 2007 soon after Danny completed the final chapter of this manuscript, the Lord called him home. Danny was 57 years old.

During a tour in Asia, while sharing his story of God's love with thousands of people, he contracted a parasite that ravaged his body beyond medical care.

However, to some degree, I feel Danny's work for God was completed here on earth, and he was ready for the place Jesus had prepared for him.

Danny's story of his incredible transformation will live on as a shining example of what God is capable of doing, and as a beacon of hope for all who call on His name.

As my brother passed from this life into the Glory of Heaven, I know that Jesus looked at him and said, "Well done, my good and faithful servant, well done."

David Velasco

Please visit

www.DetourThroughHell.org

to watch Danny's online videos, read articles, listen and download
his audio testimony so you can share his story with those in need.

CPSIA information can be obtained at www.ICGtesting.com
Printed in the USA
LVOW07s0321220916

505706LV00002B/172/P